choosing a good life

CHOOSING A
good life

◆

*Lessons from People
Who Have Found
Their Place in the World*

ALI BERMAN

HAZELDEN®

Hazelden
Center City, Minnesota 55012
hazelden.org

Library of Congress Cataloging-in-Publication Data
Berman, Ali.
   Choosing a good life : lessons from people who have found their place
in the world / Ali Berman.
     pages cm
     ISBN 978-1-61649-468-1 (paperback) — ISBN 978-1-61649-535-0 (e-book)
1. Self-actualization (Psychology) 2. Self-realization 3. Choice (Psychology)
I. Title.
   BF637.S4B473 2014
   170'.44—dc23
                                                                    2014024737

Editor's note
This publication is not intended as a substitute for the advice of health care professionals.

18 17 16 15 14   1 2 3 4 5 6

Cover design: Percolator
Interior design and typesetting: Percolator
Author photo: Gary Ploski

For Gary Ploski, Magneto, and Cthulhu

contents

acknowledgments

FIRST AND FOREMOST, thank you to Sungrai, Cathy, Emery, Zoe, Eric, Leanne, Michal, Daphne, Alex, and Lisa. I couldn't have written this book without you all. Your honesty, integrity, and how you've chosen to live your lives inspires me each day. You trusted me with your stories. I hope I was able to do them justice.

Thank you to Gary Ploski, my husband and my partner in life. You came with me to the interviews, supported me, had faith in me, and read the very first draft. You took care of so much within our own lives to give me the time I needed to write. I can never thank you enough for that. You, more than anyone else in this world, help me stay balanced by embodying so many of the traits I looked for in researching this book. Integrity, kindness, patience, gratitude—you have them all. I am so very lucky.

Thank you to Sid Farrar. Without you and your original concept, this book would not exist. You trusted a first-time author to go on this journey and helped mold it along the way.

Thank you to all the folks at Hazelden who worked so hard to make this book the best it could be, and to bring it into the world.

Thank you to Laura Strachan, my agent, for thinking of me when Sid came to you, and for having faith in me for all these years.

Thank you to David and Glenda Berman, my fantastic parents who taught me so much about being kind. I would not be who I am without your guidance and love. You are not just great parents; you are incredible people.

Thank you to Magneto and Cthulhu. You can't read this. No feline could. But you slept by my legs, rested on my arms, and purred on my stomach as I crafted this book. You kept me company and provided me daily doses of joy and contentment by being so loving and warm.

Thank you to all the friends and family who helped me find the remarkable people in this book.

Thank you to Renee Wicklund for being a fantastic friend. You read everything from the proposal to the full draft and helped to strengthen the book.

Thank you to Alexandra Branscombe for assisting me with scientific research for this book.

introduction

THREE YEARS AGO I'm sure an outside observer would have said that I was living a pretty great life. I had a healthy marriage, I loved my job, and my husband, Gary, and I had just purchased our very first house. A relationship, employment, and home ownership—all considered the modern-day building blocks of the American dream. And yet, we weren't happy. It was just the opposite; we were downright miserable.

We were exhausted by our jobs and financially crippled by a house that seemed to require a never-ending supply of money. After finding out that our newly purchased home needed a new roof, I took on a third job tutoring at night. I would wake up at 6:00 a.m., pump out an article or two as a freelance writer for job number one, go to job number two at 8:30 a.m. and finish up at 5:00 p.m., and then head to job number three. When I eventually arrived home after a very long day, all I wanted to do was to put on my pajamas, curl up with Gary (who was equally tired), and watch something on television. I wasn't working on my own writing. I wasn't reading. My friends never saw me. I barely exercised, and I ate whatever happened to be stuffed in the back of the fridge. The part of my day I looked the most forward to was bedtime. We were working as hard as we possibly could to bankroll a life that gave us little satisfaction. I wasn't living the life I wanted to, and I certainly wasn't balanced. I was getting by, and just barely.

Gary and I had dreamed of owning our own home for years, and here we were with an acre of land and 2,100 square feet beneath us. Then we learned how much it cost to heat a house during a New York winter, and we got sticker shock when we saw the price tag for a new roof. If that weren't enough, Hurricane Irene dropped four feet of water in our basement, which caused mold. Plus, having bought a house in one of the only areas we could afford, we were almost an hour away from all of our friends. That yard, the garden, and those 2,100 square feet no longer seemed like a luxury; they felt like a prison that we had to pay for. And worse yet, it was a prison of our own making.

Just a few years prior we had been the kind of people who played catch in the park, went to a midnight movie on a Thursday night, saw plays, spent time with friends, traveled, and volunteered. I loved my jobs, all three of them, but working became my entire life. Very quickly, I changed into a person who not even I wanted to be around, and Gary, who had also taken on additional work, had gone from being a jovial up-for-anything kind of guy to a more practical and sullen person. We wondered: *Where were those former versions of ourselves? What happened to them and how could we get them back?*

The daily dread I felt as I turned off the alarm and sleepwalked through the day went on for a year and a half. And then on Gary's thirty-seventh birthday, we finally reached our breaking point. Thinking back on all the financial stress, regret, and isolation we had subjected ourselves to, we turned to each other and said, nearly in unison, "We have to sell the house." That decision, to unload the split-level in Yorktown Heights, New York, and take back our lives, opened us up to new possibilities and prompted us to rethink everything. We realized that rather than spending our time and money on the things we cared about, we were spending it all on things that didn't matter to us.

Working for 90 percent of our waking hours bought us a car, furniture, and a home just outside one of the most expensive cities in the United States. But we wanted to see rain forests and mountains, make films, write books, and see plays. Wouldn't those choices bring us more joy and balance than the choices we had been making?

We were paying more than three grand a month for a house we no longer wanted and were barely using 50 percent of the space. It was time to jump ship, to stop looking for money to pay for things like water filters, a roof, and an automatic garage door opener, but never finding the funds to take that vacation or enjoy a night out at our favorite restaurant. We were living to take care of our things rather than taking care of ourselves. It was time to purge.

Six months after this realization, we put our house on the market, drove carloads of our stuff to the New Rochelle Humane Society Thrift Shop, and donated more than 600 books to the local library. We sold furniture, gave things away on Freecycle.org (an international recycling network), and wondered how much space we actually needed to live.

We kept our art, a few pieces of furniture, antiques that had been passed down from our grandmothers, and the absolute minimum number of practical necessities like dishes, cookware, and scratching posts (a must for any family with cats). I recycled my old yearbooks, parted with ticket stubs, and threw out my senior prom corsage. We didn't just go through our possessions once. We went through a series of purges. I became more brutal with each. I had thoughts like, *Yes, I love Cormac McCarthy, but maybe I'll just keep* Outer Dark *instead of half of his body of work.* Clothes? I was still holding on to things I wore in high school. Donate. That became our motto. If we weren't using it, we decided to pass it on to people who could.

By moving day we had unloaded more than half of our worldly possessions. Every box that left the house before then was another box of stuff we didn't have to move, unpack, or take care of. We could stop worrying about the next big thing in the house breaking down and costing us our entire savings. Gary was able to quit the job he had been at for eleven years and pursue his passion for film. I stopped tutoring and cut down my other hours to focus on writing again. Downsizing (the opposite of what the American dream tells us we should do) gave us options we never had before. Without all the financial obligations and with much less stuff, we finally did what we had talked about for years.

We not only left our home, we left our state. Gary and I ditched New York and headed out west to Portland, Oregon, where the cost of living was lower and the cultural values were more in line with the people we wanted to be. We traded in that 2,100-square-foot three-bedroom house and car in the suburbs for a 698-square-foot studio apartment and public transportation in the heart of the city. Rather than sitting on the couch every night, sucked into the television vortex, I read and wrote. Together, Gary and I visited mountains and waterfalls, made new friends, went to readings, spent afternoons in the park, traveled, laughed, and created memories together. I even saw my friends in New York more often, video chatting with them on a weekly basis. After years of feeling trapped, we began *doing* rather than wishing.

I had been through some rough patches before: cancer in my early twenties and a disability in my late twenties, all out of my control. My more recent struggles with the house, with working too much, and with my negative attitude—those were in my control. Gary and I had made a series of choices that had gotten us into that mess. Although it would take some work and we'd lose some money, we realized we could make different choices for our future. We could reevaluate our entire lives, ask ourselves what we really wanted, and ditch the old life that we had come to hate. We loved each other, we cared about the world, and we had passion for our work. Weren't those the true building blocks (at least for us) of a meaningful life?

It was during that time of deconstructing my life and doing my best to put it back together in a new form that I started this book. I was open. I looked with fresh eyes at my struggles and flaws: my anxiety that caused sleeplessness, my rigid nature, and my tendency to escape sometimes difficult realities by watching television (to name a few). The pieces of my life were scattered everywhere and ready to be rearranged. I was eager to learn new skills and techniques to change so many of my negative patterns.

What better way to learn how to reconstruct my life than to talk to people who had achieved what I was looking for? I knew they were out there. I just had to find them. I asked friends and acquaintances, looked through articles, and even searched on Reddit (a social networking site). I was searching for people who were flexible, who enjoyed their work, who valued their relationships with others, who prioritized having fun. I wanted to find people who had purpose, who were grateful, and who handled conflict rationally and with kindness. People who had integrity and a desire to leave the world and all its inhabitants better than they had found it. I wanted to interview those who felt good about their lives, not because they hadn't suffered (we all suffer), but because they had made adjustments that enabled them to live a balanced life in spite of that suffering.

And find those people I did. Five men and five women who ranged in age from thirty to ninety years old, born on three continents, all of whom exemplified the kind of existence I was searching for. I met with them and asked them about their lives, their choices, what drove them, and what they had learned. Each of them proved to be magnificent, telling me their life stories and how they came to be the kind of balanced individuals I think many of us are striving to become. What was even more spectacular was how much all of them had in common. How they resolve conflict, handle stress, keep their relationships strong, stay true to their personal ethics, and so much more. As I explored those commonalities I knew I had found the heart of this book and the methods I was going to implement in my own life. I felt as if I were being handed the keys to a much calmer and happier me.

The people I found hadn't lived charmed lives. They faced more difficult obstacles than I could even fathom—and I like to think of myself as a girl who has faced her fair share of demons. You name it, and someone in this book has likely experienced it. Divorce, war, illness, loss, poverty, bigotry—those are just some of the challenges they've dealt with. And yet, here they are, models of mental health, people who are excited about the world and its infinite possibilities. The rare subset of humanity that finds joy each and every day, no matter what life hurls at them. I asked questions to find out how they accomplished something so rare, the ability to stay balanced in a world that constantly throws us off center.

I learned many things about finding and maintaining balance through those conversations, perhaps most important, that balance is a moving target. Our lives change so rapidly that no one recipe works for us at every stage. What I needed at twenty-two years old was different from what I needed at thirty-two. And I'm sure that who I will be at forty-two will require me to make further adaptations. However, there are tools that work under any circumstance. Patience, kindness, gratitude, purpose, healthy living, and generosity, to name a few. Those virtues can get us through even the most tragic of times and can amplify the good in our lives. Best of all, they can help us stay balanced even when the bad overwhelms the good.

As Gary and I were going through this major change in our lives, he accompanied me on almost all of the interviews to help record them. On the way home from each, we'd reflect on what we had learned. We both felt totally inspired by the superb specimens of humanity we encountered. And on each ride home, I felt better equipped to make those important changes that would lead to a happier present and future. Gary felt the same, and together, we began to transform, to become more centered, more at peace, and more courageous; better able to pursue the things that mattered to us and more able to leave behind the things that only brought us heartache.

I believe that Sungrai, Cathy, Emery, Zoe, Eric, Leanne, Michal, Daphne, Alex, and Lisa will inspire you too. Their wisdom and their life choices encompass some of the greatest lessons humanity holds. These individuals weren't born with all the tools they have now. They acquired them over time, proving that we can all choose the kind of person we want to be.

Like the remarkable people profiled in this book, we can all take steps to make the life we envision a reality. And, fellow travelers, I hope the life lessons and tools gathered in this book help you on your own journey, just as they have helped me on mine.

EMBRACING LIFE
IN THE MIDST
OF ILLNESS

•

How does someone dealing with constant
pain and the myriad of issues surrounding
illness achieve contentment?

"Once at Mount Sinai it was extremely painful. I couldn't
think. I had many helpers at Mount Sinai and especially
one person—we were very close. She would always check
on me when I was there. So I asked her to sing anything
and that just eased my pain. And she was just singing
through the night, you know, any time she would come
back and that just really helped me."

—*Sungrai Sohn*

chapter 1

Sungrai,

a Master of the Violin and the "State of Flow"

THE GROUNDS WERE THE FIRST THING I noticed when I arrived at sixty-two-year-old Sungrai Sohn's home in Suffern, New York. It was late July 2013, and although the previous week was dry from a record-breaking heat wave, Sungrai's property was lush, with meticulously groomed gardens in every direction I looked. The gardener in me was instantly in awe, not just because of their masterful design, but because his entire property, with its huge ponds, mature willow trees, and forest, was a sight to behold. A deer peered out at us from behind the pond, and large koi swam beneath the surface. Later, Sungrai informed me that the animals are all so used to his presence that they look at him with idle interest rather than flying, running, or paddling away. His home is a sanctuary for all beings.

Sungrai had been outside all day weeding. The kale and rainbow chard were in perfect rows. If you looked at his tomato plants, you wouldn't find a single yellow leaf. Their absence can be attributed to his unwavering attention—he plucks any and all imperfections as they happen. If it's hot, he's outside at 7:00 a.m. If it's cooler, he could be out there all day. However, it's not his need for orderly kale that makes him work so hard. It's because at any moment his phone might ring and he'll have to leave his home and his garden for an unknown period of time. Maybe forever. Sungrai Sohn is waiting for a liver transplant. His second. And this time they aren't sure if he'll make it, and if he does, how long the painful recovery process will take.

He and his wife, Patricia, had invited my husband, Gary, and me for dinner before the interview, and when we entered their home, I was taken aback by one simple action. Sungrai hugged me. Knowing that he's susceptible to getting sick due to his weakened immune system, I was prepared to keep a bit of a distance. I didn't expect a handshake and certainly no hug. I was so surprised when he reached out with both arms that it must have shown on my face, and the somewhat awkward embrace that followed was due to my being unprepared and scared that I might breathe on him. I didn't feel sick, but what if I were incubating something? That was *my* concern, not his. Sungrai takes necessary precautions to keep healthy, but he doesn't lock himself in a bubble or worry about getting sick. He lives his life fully, enjoying what was then about ten years of extra time.

He told me that when it comes to his health, "No, I don't worry. I didn't worry even the second time [I was hospitalized] after I thought I wasn't going to make it." He explained, "I was at peace because I did everything I wanted to do and more. I did all the things as best as I could."

That's why his garden is always in order. If everything is taken care of to the best of his ability, he doesn't have to worry about it. No use thinking when one could be *doing*. And Sungrai is a doer, someone who takes action—he has that in common with everyone I interviewed for this book.

After dinner, Sungrai and I went into his soundproofed music room that contains a variety of exquisite violins, a piano, and beautiful antiques. I asked him, a little shyly, if after the interview he would mind playing a short piece for me. This is a request he gets a lot, but he humored me and said yes. Sungrai says yes to as many invitations as he can, but playing the violin—an art form he has spent his life perfecting—is something he doesn't do as if it's just some party trick. He usually reserves it for practicing or playing for crowds rather than for individuals. It's both his passion and his tool for earning his living, so he is protective of this part of his life. I settled into the interview knowing that afterward I would be in for a rare treat.

As we both set ourselves up on the couch and chair in front of the piano, I started our interview with what I considered to be the very beginning of the story: the day Sungrai discovered the violin.

When the now master was a mere four years old in his native country of Korea, Sungrai's father, an importer/exporter, brought home a movie poster that would steer the direction of Sungrai's life. "The poster—we had posters everywhere at home—had Gary Cooper playing a violin and poking somebody's eye," he told me. "So I thought, wow, that is cool. I'm going to do that. And as soon as they heard that I wanted to play violin, my father went to Japan and bought a trunk full of music and a violin. And my mother was a concert pianist. She found the best teacher, and there I was playing at four years old."

By the time he was six, Sungrai was playing on Korean television. The doctors believe he contracted hepatitis B during childhood—maybe from the wet nurse his father enlisted when they ran out of milk on the train from Seoul to Pusan at the start of the Korean war, maybe from the communal eating style common at many dinner tables at the time. They just aren't sure. They do know that hepatitis B has given him lifelong and life-threatening health problems.

In 2001, Sungrai's health was deteriorating fast. He was cold all the time, even when deep under heavy blankets and sweaters. His memory was fading, and he was unable to sleep. He was on the list to receive a liver transplant, but although he was very ill, he was not on the top of the list—there were people ahead of him who were doing even worse. Sungrai had to wait and hope that his turn would come and that when it finally arrived, he'd be strong enough to make it through the surgery. It was around that time that Patricia's brother David and his wife read an article in the *New York Times* about living donors. As soon as David read the article, he knew he wanted to donate a lobe of his liver to his brother-in-law to save his life.

At first, Sungrai and Patricia were hesitant. They hadn't even been told that getting a donation from a friend or relative was possible. And, as with any surgery, there were risks to the donor. But David and his wife were adamant. David went through the tests, both psychological and physical, and he passed with flying colors. When the social worker asked him in a variety of ways if he was being coerced or pressured into donating, he said, "Just the opposite. I was pressuring to become a live donor."

The surgery was scheduled soon after David was cleared. To the relief of everyone, it was a great success. For the first time in years

Sungrai woke up feeling warm. His head was clear and he finally had a working liver again. Without that donation, Sungrai's doctor told him that he would have only lived for another month. At the time of our interview, David's gift had already added ten plus years to Sungrai's life and serves as a constant reminder that selflessness and love can indeed save lives.

For years Sungrai lived his life feeling renewed. He still suffered from hepatitis B, but the working liver allowed him to live a relatively normal existence. Unfortunately, the bile ducts within the donor liver were problematic, causing chronic cholangitis (a bacterial infection of the bile duct). They tried to fix the issue with a second surgery, but without success. Now, Sungrai needs another liver. This time a living donor won't do. He needs the full organ instead of a single lobe. Once again, he is near the top of the UNOS (United Network for Organ Sharing) list.

ONE MIGHT ASSUME THAT SUNGRAI would be devastated that he has to go through all of this again. It's just the opposite. As he explained it, all of the time he has had since his first transplant has been a gift. And he's made sure every moment has been utilized. It might sound cliché, but Sungrai has truly mastered the ability to live in the moment, giving 100 percent to everything he does. Sungrai has kept busy immersing himself in the things he loves, whether it's teaching at Sarah Lawrence College, gardening, spending time with his wife and family, playing concerts around the world, or learning something new each year, like wind surfing, flying an airplane, or riding a motorcycle, just to name a few of his hobbies.

It was a pleasure to sit down and speak with the soft-spoken man. He was spending his summer at home since he always had to be, at a moment's notice, within a four-hour drive from Mount Sinai Hospital in case a liver became available. He's quick to smile and laugh, even when talking about his illness.

SUNGRAI WAS MY FIRST INTERVIEW for this book, and exactly the kind of person I was looking for. When I initially learned about Sungrai, it wasn't his illness that made me reach out to him. Many of his personality traits drew me to him, but one in particular made me desperately want to meet him. Even though I'm not sure he had ever heard the term, Sungrai's dedication to the violin, his hobbies, and his acute interest in so many other things had made him an expert in something known in the positive psychology field as "flow," the exhilarating feeling of being so absorbed in something that the rest of the world seems to disappear. You've probably experienced this state quite often yourself but never knew it had a name. "Flow," a term coined by psychologist Mihaly Csikszentmihalyi, has been defined as "the creative moment when a person is completely involved in an activity for its own sake."

Shortly before his first transplant, Sungrai had a trip planned to perform in Korea, something he had done with his quartet mates for years. It took an incredible amount of planning and coordination to schedule the annual tour. Sungrai didn't want to disappoint his colleagues so he kept his commitment, even though he had nowhere near his full strength. One might think that because of his weakened state, his performance wouldn't be up to its normal standards. Despite being in pain, when he got on stage to play, nothing else mattered but the music. When he was "in flow," he wasn't sick. He wasn't suffering. He existed in a small pocket of time where nothing else mattered but the music. He told me, "When you're on the stage, you forget things and adrenaline is running. You forget—which is a good thing."

Whatever Sungrai does, whether it's gardening, playing a concert, fixing up his vintage Austin-Healey convertible, or even teaching, he does it with his full attention on the task at hand. He describes his relationship with flow when he's playing the violin by saying, "I don't think about anything else, just the music."

Perhaps you participated in sports in school and remember the feeling of playing so hard that you could no longer hear the crowd. Maybe you executed a difficult maneuver and you don't even recall making any decisions. Your body and mind reacted in unison to give you the ability to make something happen—something that you might not have been able to achieve had you not been enjoying that beautiful state of flow. A pastry chef might feel the same thing while decorating a cake, or a comedian as she does stand-up on stage, or a dancer in the ballet.

Sungrai's days are filled with activities he loves. He plays his violin, teaches students, and commits to learning new things all the time so he can be challenged to explore the world with his own hands, his own heart, his own mind. Time moves differently in flow state. On the days that he spends hours upon hours in his garden tending to the plants he loves, he says he barely notices that time is moving. He doesn't depend on outside stimuli to bring him joy. He finds it himself by doing. Sungrai's life is a verb. He is always active.

Csikszentmihalyi writes, "We can be happy experiencing the passive pleasure of a rested body, warm sunshine, or the contentment of a serene relationship, but this kind of happiness is very vulnerable and dependent on favorable external circumstances. The happiness that follows flow is of our own making, and it leads to increasing complexity and growth in consciousness."[1]

Think about how many minutes per day you spend in a flow state. When you get home from work, are you doing something? Cooking, woodworking, sewing, fixing a car, writing? Or is it a Bravo reality television marathon? (No judgment. Okay, a little judgment.) If it's the latter, you might want to consider challenging your body and mind more regularly. Turn off the television and turn to your favorite hobby.

This ability to constantly learn new skills and take part in the activities he loves has not just brought Sungrai joy; it has also helped him cope with the excruciating pain he has had to endure during his life. In the scientific community, the act of focusing on something calming and comforting in an effort to relieve some of the stress of chronic illness is called *distraction*. Sungrai can't windsurf when he's ill. He can use his mental focus to visualize a safe and pleasant experience from childhood, a tactic he utilized when the pain was so intense that he had trouble sleeping. The trick is to busy the mind—to distract oneself—with anything other than the seemingly never-ending feelings of discomfort. If the mind stays busy on something enjoyable, pain becomes easier to bear. Sungrai, for sure, has a busy mind.

Distraction, in the world of happiness research, has a lot in common with flow. I would argue that Sungrai's mastering of flow has helped him handle the cycles of pain he's endured for decades. Whether it was during the time when he was perpetually cold, or when he was recovering from his liver surgeries, or during his more recent battles with illness, Sungrai has always had music and sound as a sanctuary to retreat to when not even medicine could dull the pain.

His interest in sound began as a young boy. His mother told him he had been a quiet child. Perhaps this was because Sungrai was always listening. It's not just the violin that comforts him. It could be the insects and birds out in his garden, or a voice singing. Sungrai recalled, "Once at Mount Sinai it was extremely painful. I couldn't think. I had many helpers at Mount Sinai and especially one person—we were very close. She would always check on me when I was there. So I asked her to sing anything and that just eased my pain. And she was just singing through the night, you know, any time she would come back and that just really helped me. So it's not just violin. You can take so many pills and sometimes they don't even work because you passed that point. And so somebody like that just eased my pain."

Sungrai described teaching as another wonderful and productive method of distracting himself. He told me, "You know, you forget you are sick when you are teaching. And that really saved me through all the illness and all the pain."

The master violinist has been teaching at Sarah Lawrence College for thirty years. He recently taught violin and viola, chamber music, string orchestra, sight reading for instrumentalists, and master classes. All of that with a compromised liver. He said the pleasure comes from watching a student who has been struggling finally figure something out: "When they understand what I'm trying to do and suddenly get it—the satisfaction of that is real joy."

In fact, when I asked him what brings him the most joy in his life, he told me that right now, teaching is at the top of his list. When Sungrai is working with a student, he said his identity is that of a teacher, not of a sick man. He's responsible for the education of others, a duty he takes very seriously. When someone is sick and visiting doctor after doctor, it can be easy to let the normal world fall away and feel owned by his or her failing body. Sungrai has done absolutely the opposite. He has maintained his rich world in spite of his illness.

The condition of his health is just one more facet of who he is. It's not the defining one.

Although I don't know what it's like to spend decades struggling with hepatitis B and a failing liver, I do have an intimate and complex history with pain. I spent most of my twenties dealing with thyroid cancer and disabling foot problems. After Sungrai described his tactics for getting through the worst moments, I remembered using many of them myself. When doctors first suspected I had thyroid cancer, they had to take a biopsy to be sure. I'm a team player so I employed my good old standby deep breathing techniques and forced jokes to keep calm while a very long needle was stuck into the center of my neck. Unfortunately, the nodule was too hard for the needle to grab a sufficient number of cells, so that first biopsy turned up nothing. They brought me back, had a pathologist on standby, and did it again. Seventeen times. Seventeen needles going straight into my neck as I did everything in my power to distract myself from the ever-worsening pain. The first needle? Not so bad. Every needle after that was more painful than the one before. And even worse than the biopsy needle was the burning anesthetic that they kept pumping into the area. In those moments and the many that followed before and after surgery, had I not been able to take control of my mind and focus on my body, on my breathing, I would have been running out the door.

As Sungrai discovered, being ill is often a full-time job. It's not just the pain that he got so good at dealing with; he also had to manage the never-ending doctor appointments, the procedures, the insurance problems, and the scheduling. With the help of his wife and family, Sungrai has mastered living with a chronic condition.

So how does someone dealing with constant pain and the myriad of issues surrounding illness achieve contentment? For the able-bodied person whose worst experience with physical suffering is the annual February sniffles or a badly stubbed toe, the ideas of living in pain and being at peace probably seem contrary. If pain is always present, how does the mind make room for joy? Sungrai has done this by learning how to manage his pain through distraction, engaging his flow state, spending time with friends and family, and accepting his condition. Acceptance doesn't mean he has stopped fighting. Sungrai makes it clear that he wants to live. He wants his phone to ring with the news of a donor so that he might be given the chance to watch his grandchildren grow up. But in spite of his deep desire to live, Sungrai fully enjoys his time in the present. When he's well, he fills his days with antiquing trips with his wife, time outside in nature, and, of course, playing the violin and arranging music. Pain is a part of his life, as is the threat of liver failure, but those two realities don't negate his other, even greater, reality. He enjoys his life and is thankful for what he has.

Part of what keeps him so engaged with the world is something he figured out early on—that being a lifelong learner benefits him in incalculable ways. The violin was his first love, both playing music and teaching it, but he also knew he wanted to branch out and look for interests totally outside of his professional life. He said, "When I was in my second year in college, I said I have to do something else. That's when I started searching to find what's really out there to learn. So I went to the airport, a local tiny little airport. I said, 'I want to fly. Anybody going up?' And one guy said, 'Yeah, I'm going up. Would you like to come?' So I did that for many times with that particular person. And then when I started touring, if I have time I just go to the local airport and I just fly with whoever is going up. So that is one way I started learning new things."

He continued, "People are so generous. When you ask them, they'll teach you how to do things; and that's how I thought maybe I should do this every year, learn something new." Sungrai hasn't stopped. And some of the things he has learned have become lifelong hobbies and interests.

ONE OF THE THINGS I FOUND most fascinating about Sungrai came out during a conversation we had about worrying. I'm talking about the kind of worry that keeps a person up at night, the kind that rules their thoughts and emotions and makes it impossible to focus on anything else—a sensation I'm fluent in. You'd think a man like Sungrai who is constantly waiting for the phone to ring, whose illness could take a serious nosedive any day, would always be on edge, overcome with anxiety. He's exactly the opposite. He sleeps soundly. He said his head hits the pillow and that's that until morning. He's able to accomplish this remarkable feat because this magical man doesn't feel worry the same way that I do. And his solution to the worry problem is also how he's been able to live with no regrets.

Sungrai said he received some of the best advice in his life when he was studying at Sarah Lawrence with his mentor Dorothy De-Lay. "She said, 'A lot of people worry so much. Before the concert they worry. After the concert they worry.' And she said, 'But that didn't help anybody. Why worry? Instead of wasting time worrying, do something about it.' And I took that into my heart. So instead of worrying about it, I just go ahead and do things. If I have to learn something, I go ahead and learn it instead of worrying about it. So she really helped me in a professional way, and that really got into a lot of other things, life in general."

Sungrai's advice is among the best I heard during the interviews I did for this book. If he thinks he may be able to effect change in a given situation, he works as hard as possible, giving it his all, to influence the outcome. At that point, even if he fails, he knows that he has done his best. He believes that if one always works as hard as they can, there is no room for regret in a life. I like to think of it this way: If I have a test coming up and study a moderate amount but know I could have worked harder, I might get a C, but I'd feel like I could have earned a higher grade. However, if I study for a test and fully dedicate myself to learning the material, giving it my very best effort, and still get that C, well, that's a different feeling. At that point, someone with Sungrai's outlook on life would probably shrug

Study after study has shown that people who are prone to worrying have higher and earlier mortality rates than those who have learned how to curb this behavior. Dan Mroczek, an associate professor of child development and family studies at Purdue University, concluded through his research that those he labeled as neurotic (meaning people who are prone to worrying; feeling excessive amounts of anxiety or depression) died sooner than their less stressed peers. Mroczek said about his research, "We found that neurotic men whose levels dropped over time had a better chance at living longer. They seemed to recover from any damage high levels of the trait may have caused. On the flip side, neurotic men whose neuroticism increased over time died much sooner than their peers."[2]

and say something to the effect of, "Well, I tried my best. No regrets. No worries." For a man like Sungrai, with chronic health problems, being able to set aside worries goes far in safeguarding his health.

Ever since my interview with Sungrai, I think of him when I have problems and how he works as hard as he possibly can to come up with a solution, then acts on it. I try to emulate his behavior. If something needs to be addressed, I do it then and there instead of procrastinating. That way, it doesn't take up unnecessary space in my mind. As I said at the beginning of this story, no use stewing when one could be doing. Give it a try. Sungrai hit the jackpot with that realization, and over the past forty or so years, it appears to have served him exceptionally well. Little seems to bother him, not even money problems.

As many of us know (often all too well), money troubles are one of the most stressful issues a person can face. Perhaps that's why many who have never had a lot of extra money (including me), dream of winning the lottery or inheriting a huge sum from some long-forgotten relative. Around many dinner tables one might hear, "If I were rich, I would . . ." Fill in the blank. Quit my job. Buy a big house. Go on a trip around the world. Some have the opposite experience. They start out with money, and then lose it all. That's what happened to Sungrai's family.

Despite a tumultuous start during the Korean war, Sungrai grew up in a big house with servants and drivers. It didn't last. As he described it, "A lot of repressive political things happened, so my father ended up in jail and lost everything." Sungrai came to the United States on a scholarship and his family came too, all of them starting over in a new country. While in school, Sungrai struggled financially, sometimes even having trouble finding enough for food. He only had enough to pay for six months of dorm housing and then had to find a room to rent off campus. Those were difficult times for him. Less so for his father.

Sungrai explained, "For my father, he said, 'I'm free. I don't have to chase money anymore. I have enough money I can live on. I'm happy.'" His life in America, where he no longer had to maintain the lavish lifestyle the family had once enjoyed, ended up giving him a chance to relish life again. Sungrai continued, "My father was working probably 24/7. I never saw him in Korea. But when he came here, my mother and my father got so close. My mother said, 'It's like a second honeymoon now.'"

It took a bit longer for Sungrai to see the good in losing so much financial security. But he eventually learned that having to make a life for himself was more valuable than having the world handed to him. And knowing that he was able to make it even though he had no money, no comforts, is a badge he wears proudly. He told me, "If someone gave me a lot of money all the time, I don't think I'd be here. But because I did survive by myself, if somebody takes all this, I know I can survive again. For me it was a blessing in a way."

For those of us who have never experienced the pampering available to those with extreme wealth, the idea of financial freedom can be especially alluring. We might believe that more money means more happiness, because, of course, money buys things. Money means less stress and, we think, more fun. For Sungrai's father, however, working to make enough money for that luxurious lifestyle meant not spending time with his family. Losing it all gave him a freedom he hadn't known before.

During the time when Sungrai was broke, he knew of only one way to support himself—with his violin. Once he had made enough

How much money does a person actually need to be happy? Turns out, some researchers were able to put a number on it. In 2010, Daniel Kahneman and Angus Deaton released a study showing that once a person reached an earning level of about $75,000, their happiness no longer increased with more money. Their life evaluation, meaning the way they reflect upon their life as a whole, may have improved upon earning more funds, but emotional well-being during day-to-day life? That hardly budged. Deaton and Kahneman write, "We conclude that lack of money brings both emotional misery and low life evaluation; similar results were found for anger. Beyond $75,000 in the contemporary United States, however, higher income is neither the road to experienced happiness nor the road to the relief of unhappiness or stress, although higher income continues to improve individuals' life evaluations."[3]

money to fulfill his most basic needs, he stopped equating art with money. He said, "That was just sheer making money, but I want to make music." A fine distinction.

I realize there is a vast difference in the levels of happiness between someone making $4,000 a year and someone making $40,000. When one is worrying about where their next meal will come from, happiness is hard to achieve. Sungrai faced that very problem while in college. After he was able to earn enough to fill his stomach and keep adequate shelter, he flourished without chasing a higher income. As his father learned, money does not make a happy life. All the drivers, servants, and wealth he had attained in Korea became nothing more than a lifestyle he was forced to maintain by working long hours away from his family. A person creates a balanced life through their relationships, passions, and daily experiences. Money is necessary to take care of yourself and your family, but unnecessary riches? They won't make you closer to your friends or more connected with your children.

PEOPLE WHO LIVE A GOOD LIFE aren't immune to the normal ups and downs. They still feel the full spectrum of human emotions. Unlike me (and maybe you), they don't dwell in their negative emotions. If something bad happens, people like Sungrai are able to rebound faster than the typical person.

Most would say that Sungrai has the right to be sad, depressed, angry, or any combination thereof after spending so many years fighting for his life. He doesn't seem to be any of those things. When I asked him how he handled getting disappointing news, he told me, "I think I'm generally a happy person because I don't get depressed really. I thought I was depressed a few days ago, because why aren't they calling me for surgery? Time is up. Come on, let's do it. And then I thought, *Am I hoping someone will die?* And then I felt really bad. That took about five minutes of depression I guess and then I started getting busy again so I forgot everything."

What Sungrai is describing is something called the "Hedonic treadmill," the idea that good and bad life events might impact our emotional state for a period of time, but that we will always return to our baseline. Sungrai felt momentarily upset that his phone had not yet rung. Why wasn't it his turn? Hadn't he waited patiently long enough? He then realized that his desire for a new liver to save his life was directly linked to the death of another person. And this made him feel even worse. Not only had he not received a donated liver; he was, in some ways, hoping for another person to die so that he could live. That insight was enough to make him feel, as he said, "really bad." How long did it last? Five minutes. Then, Sungrai's negative emotions bounced back up to his normal level of happiness. As he said, he got "busy again." He didn't—and doesn't—dwell on what he can't control. No navel gazing. He's far too busy to sit wondering or worrying.

It's not as if someone dented his car or he stubbed his toe, small life events that would momentarily disrupt his emotional state. The man is waiting for a liver. His own liver is failing. His continued life is directly dependent on the death of another human being. If he stayed in bed for a week listening to sad music with a pint of ice cream in his hand, I don't think anyone would judge him. But that's simply not how his mind reacts to negative stimuli. Sungrai instinctively chooses to think of all the positives in his life rather than indulge in the difficulties. Focusing on the good things leaves him feeling exceptionally grateful, an emotion that helps him appreciate what he has rather than lamenting what he doesn't have.

At the dinner table before we started eating, Patricia asked if we were religious. Gary and I responded no, but said that we have no problem with a prayer. She thought about it and told us that she's not necessarily praying to God. It's more the act of saying out loud all the things that she is grateful for that she finds so important.

Sungrai was much the same. When we spoke, he kept talking about all the people in his life who have helped get him to where he is today. His parents who he loved dearly. His wife who accompanies him to work each day just in case the phone happens to ring and they need to get to the hospital. The doctors and caregivers in his life who have helped him survive. His brother-in-law who donated a lobe of his liver. Sungrai is surrounded by goodness in the people he chooses to have in his life.

One of the hardest parts of practicing gratitude or getting up to do something new is that our negative emotions can at times feel like a cage with no exit. That can even be true when we know what tools would make us feel better. The important thing to remember is that getting up and forcing ourselves to do something, even when we'd rather stay in bed, is one of the best ways to help us regain our mental equilibrium. It takes discipline and practice. The more we do it, the more firsthand proof we will have that it works, and the next time, we'll be able to get up faster. For those of us who don't have Sungrai's natural abilities to rebound, we have to push ourselves a little bit harder.

AT THE END OF THE EVENING, as the interview was winding down, I got my wish. In addition to the natural high I was experiencing from learning so much and from being around such a positive person (it's proven that being around positive people makes you more positive!), Sungrai was going to play for me. He took out an exquisite looking violin, tucked the instrument under his chin, and created some of the most beautiful sounds I had ever heard. His eyes were closed as he played the Andante cantabile by Tchaikovsky. Gary and I sat listening, watching his fingers and the bow move perfectly in sync. What a treat. Not only was I listening to the music of a master, I was also witnessing Sungrai's flow state, the place that has brought him balance and peace since he was a child in Korea. Fifty-eight years later and it's still just as important.

While Sungrai played I thought about how I would go home and put into practice so many of the things he talked about. I felt better equipped to handle my anxiety and some of the sleep issues I had been having. I was going through a period of waking up for an hour or two every night between 3:00 and 4:00 a.m., which left me exhausted during the day. But now I had new tools to stop my brain from obsessing over the fifty things it was tossing about within its walls. And I knew that the lessons I learned that night were only the beginning. I still had nine more people to talk to who would tell me about the keys that had helped them achieve balanced lives and provide clues on how the rest of us can accomplish the same remarkable feat.

ON FEBRUARY 28, 2014, the day before we moved to Portland, Oregon, I went to visit Sungrai in his office. It was seven months after our interview, and he was still waiting for his phone to ring. He looked wonderful when I saw him, but just two months earlier had spent weeks in the hospital, in pain and unsure of his fate. That's Sungrai's reality. He doesn't know what tomorrow will bring. He only knows that he has to value today, because it truly is precious.

During that lovely chat in his office, he told me something I didn't know, that his diagnosis was what prompted him to change the way he lived his life. His illness has caused him pain and years of struggle, but it's also given him an incredible gift. Sungrai has lived more fully than almost anyone I know since he learned he had hepatitis B. He doesn't put things off until tomorrow. Tomorrow he might be sick or get a call from Mount Sinai. Today matters because that's where he is right now. Planning for the future is important, but the present is the only place any of us can live our lives. It took a life-threatening chronic illness to help shape Sungrai's outlook on life. The truth is no one gets a guarantee that they will live to be 100, or that the life they lead now will be the same life they lead tomorrow. Adopting Sungrai's philosophy—to always do your best, not to worry, to make each day matter, and to never procrastinate—is something I hope we all do. I know it's already helped me in immeasurable ways.

ON MAY 8, 2014, nine and a half months after our interview and more than a year and a half after he was put on the list, Sungrai received a call from the hospital. They had a liver for him. The very next day, Sungrai underwent a five-hour surgery. One of his doctors said once it was complete, "It wasn't a good surgery, it was a perfect surgery." On May 16, Sungrai returned home to his family.

NOURISHING
OUR GIFTS

•

How do childhood passions
shape the lives we choose?

"When I was a child, I can remember walking to school and talking with everybody, whether it was the most popular kid in school or whether it was the kid whom everybody picked on. I just talked to everybody because in my heart I just enjoyed doing that. And then I found people would talk to me about personal things that they didn't talk to other people about. And that stroked my ego I'd say, but it also connected me. I felt helpful. They had an ear; they had someone to talk to, someone who could listen and not judge. I didn't know that's what it was called at the time, but I didn't judge them. I would always imagine what it's like to live in their situation. How would I feel? So that kind of was my life's work laid out before me, but I didn't know what to call it."

—*Cathy McInerney*

chapter 2

Cathy,

a Marriage and Family Therapist
Who Became Who She Always Was

When I was a child, I loved three things: writing, animals, and nature. I spent hours down by the pond searching for tadpoles, salamanders, and rare flowers. I was inspired by the tiniest of insects, wanting to see and visit their worlds, even if just for a short time. When I wasn't outside climbing up my favorite Japanese maple, I experimented with writing styles: journal entries, short stories, and editorials. I found personal satisfaction as I crafted together arguments or created a character. Writing, animals, and nature—those were the building blocks of who I was. They weren't childish interests; they were the earliest signs of what my lifelong passions would be, as long as I nourished them. As long as I didn't dismiss them simply because I was growing up.

Today, I like to think I'm the same as my girlhood self—that younger Ali. Who I was then is who I am now. Sure, there are fewer flannel shirts, and I'm thankfully not nearly as awkward (most of the time). I still like to watch cicadas in the garden, spend hours figuring out the right next line for a poem, and smell the freshness of horse manure and hay. Keeping true to those earliest passions is why, as an adult, I still have passion in my life. I never put away those childish things.

For Sungrai, it was the violin. For others with whom I spoke, it was something else that began in their childhood, something that stood outside of their relationships with friends and family that only they could offer the world. Some, like Sungrai, found their gifts at an early age and others took longer to figure it out. But all of them discovered the origins of their future passions as children. And even more important, they allowed those interests to determine what they would do as adults. In a way, they all still get to play for a living.

I found no greater example of this beautiful phenomenon than with fifty-nine-year-old Cathy McInerney, a marriage and family therapist who lives in Connecticut. Because of the nature of her work, Cathy understands herself in a way that no other person I interviewed seemed to. She sees so clearly how events and relationships molded her, and she was able to give me the timeline of her life so I, too, could see how all of these events led to where she is now. She is a fascinating woman who obviously loves the inner and outer world she has built—a world that began with her earliest memories of helping others.

WHEN CATHY MCINERNEY was in the fourth grade, a boy in her class confided in her that he *liked* a girl. He needed advice, and Cathy, he thought, was just the right nine-year-old to ask to help. Cathy told me she clearly remembers how she felt that day at Edison School so many years ago. There she was, younger than the rest of her class, put into school a year early and always feeling behind academically. Then, incredibly, she was being asked to assist this boy with his crush. Little Kenny must have seen something inside her that told him, "This is a person who can be trusted. This is a person who can keep my secrets and offer me sound advice." If so, Kenny was right. By asking her for help, he had in a way helped Cathy discover what she wanted to do for the rest of her life (although she wouldn't figure this out herself for nearly two decades).

From as early as Cathy can remember, even before Kenny's romantic troubles, she had always been a confidant to others. She told me, "When I was a child, I can remember walking to school and talking with everybody, whether it was the most popular kid in school or whether it was the kid whom everybody picked on. I just talked to everybody because in my heart I just enjoyed doing that. And then I found people would talk to me about personal things that they didn't talk to other people about. And that stroked my ego I'd say, but it also connected me. I felt helpful. They had an ear; they had someone to talk to, someone who could listen and not judge. I didn't know that's what it was called at the time, but I didn't judge them. I would always imagine what it's like to live in their situation. How would I feel? So that kind of was my life's work laid out before me, but I didn't know what to call it."

Researchers at the University of California, Riverside, the Oregon Research Institute, and the University of Oregon found that personality traits observed in childhood are a strong predictor of adult behavior.[4] By recording behavioral data on 2,400 elementary school–aged children in the 1960s and then doing follow-up research on 144 of those same subjects forty years later, the researchers were able to see how personality traits largely stayed the same. Lead author on the paper, Christopher S. Nave, concluded, "We remain recognizably the same person. This speaks to the importance of understanding personality because it does follow us wherever we go across time and contexts."

Cathy said she was a great listener for others, but that she spent her childhood without having a "Cathy" of her own. She was very selective about those with whom she shared her innermost thoughts. As the middle child of three sisters within a large (and nosy) Italian family, she said she always felt as if she were under the microscope, so she worked hard to carve out an identity of her own. Cathy told me, "Everybody was in everybody else's business. So no matter what move you made, someone else would find out about it. Whether it was positive or negative, somebody always had a comment about it. So I always felt scrutinized and I would say that I experienced anxiety because of that."

Cathy reacted to her family life by keeping her inner life private, allowing her deepest thoughts to be hers alone. She took solace in assisting others with their problems and acting as a trusted friend to anyone who needed one. Whether they were popular or unpopular, Cathy always treated her fellow classmates with kindness. She recounted an experience of sitting next to a girl in school when they were very young: "We were in first or second grade and she had problems eliminating, so kids would make fun of her. Then she got placed next to me. We were sitting side by side and she said to me, 'Are you going to make fun of me because of what happens?' And I said, 'No, I feel kind of bad. You know, if you can't control it you can't control it.' So our friendship grew from that. But she was afraid that I might be like some of those other people. So we stayed side by side for the whole year."

This ability to show kindness even as a young child, to not judge others, and not pick on those who were more vulnerable, shows just how remarkable Cathy was and is. Perhaps some of Cathy's compassion for others came from her own feeling that she "didn't quite measure up." Placed in kindergarten when she was only four (without the benefit of being a child prodigy), she spent her school-age years always working to catch up. As high school graduation approached, she decided that for the time being she had had enough with school. A college education was the last thing she wanted to pursue. Struggling for all those years led her to believe that she would have failed at college anyway.

Cathy needed time to get to know herself as an adult outside of her identity as a student, a sister, and a daughter. She had to learn who she was independent of all those entities before she could really begin to open up and gain confidence. After high school, she began working at a finance company. She also met the love of her life, Michael, the first person with whom she truly shared her inner world. He went to college while she worked, and they married when she was twenty-one. She told me about her relationship, "I've allowed people to come into my life through my relationship with my husband. You know, through a loving trusting relationship, healing takes place. Change occurs. I shared a lot with him, more so than with others at that time."

Now outside of the fishbowl that was her family life, Cathy was able to develop her identity as the independent person she had craved to be as a child. She went back to school to learn shorthand and typing and found that her relationship with school had changed. Instead of always being the one who was behind, Cathy excelled—much to her own surprise. She soon found a job at General Electric, making twice the money she had been earning at the finance company.

Cathy told me that as she approached her late twenties, she

experienced one of the most defining moments in her life when her father died. She believed that she was handling the loss, unaware that a dark cloud had settled over her. She didn't know she was depressed. She only knew that her body and temperament were changing. She said, "I wasn't sleeping at night. I had put on weight. I was not really taking care of myself. I really didn't care how I looked when I went to work. It was really burdensome in the morning to get up and take a shower and put on my makeup. I'd probably say it was situational depression. My sister was visiting for Christmas and I was very irritable with her. She said, 'I think you need to go see somebody' and I said, 'For what?' and she said, 'Well you're not sleeping at night and you're irritable.' So I thought, *Okay, I'll go.*"

Cathy was twenty-nine when she went to therapy and found a safe space to recover from the loss of her father. During her sessions other things began to open up within her. She said, "That was a game changer actually for me because when I went to this therapist, it was all about me. It wasn't about me and my sisters. It wasn't about me and my mother. I felt really good, going through a discovery there and finding out that according to his assessment, I *didn't* grieve my father and I had no idea there was a possibility for that. You know, so my eyes opened."

It wasn't just personal discovery that inspired Cathy during this time. She said she also realized that there were actually jobs doing exactly what she had been doing since she was a child—helping others through attentive listening and talking to them. She saw how powerful this could be and said she found herself wanting to do for others what her therapist had done for her in the wake of her father's death. She explained, "I think therapy was probably three months, but I was a sponge. I was there, I was interested, I was open to what was happening in the process and I wanted to do that for someone else."

Cathy's life changed quickly after that. At thirty-two, between having her first and second child, she started college with the goal of becoming a therapist. By taking one class per semester year-round, Cathy finished her bachelor's degree in twelve years. She graduated when she was forty-four.

During those years, Cathy became a multitasking expert. She said, "I was able to work around family schedules, like the kids' sports and homework. When I look back at it, it's like, *I'm phenomenal!* But when I was going through it, I was just, *How am I going to make this work? This is what I want to do. I want my kids to have a happy childhood. I want us to be a good family.*" By taking things slowly, she was able to do it all. She worked part time, was there for her children, sometimes doing her homework at the same time as they did theirs, yet still managed to graduate from college cum laude.

That still wasn't the end of her academic journey. She went on to graduate school and after an academic career that spanned eighteen years, Cathy finally earned her master's degree. At the age of fifty, when most people are starting to wind down their careers and start dreaming of retirement, she became a licensed marriage and family therapist. She now makes a living doing what she did so freely all her life: she listens to others without judgment to help them with their problems.

The incredible thing about Cathy's story is that being a therapist— that act of living her dream—is just a part of what makes her perfect for this book. It was in the act of *becoming*, going through those eighteen years of schooling and learning about herself during the process, that she really evolved into the balanced individual she is today. She's not someone who was born comfortable in her own skin. She doubted herself and had trouble taking in constructive criticism. She wasn't able to confide in others (even though they so freely confided in her). She had anxiety and felt scrutinized by her family. There were many obstacles for her to overcome. Through half a lifetime of learning and self-reflection, she let go of so much that had been holding her back.

By the time she was done recounting the significant events of her life, I was tearing up. I said to her, "I'm so happy for you. When I think of what things were like for you as a child and who you have become, I just think, you've come so far and it's wonderful."

It was during her master's program that Cathy let go of so many negative emotions. She took part in something called Gestalt training, an experiential form of psychotherapy. Cathy and her classmates didn't just learn theory. They practiced on one another, alternating time as therapist and patient while their peers observed. For someone like Cathy, who as a child felt like her life was constantly being dissected, this was a difficult process at first. She almost quit after the first year. She recalled, "In the Gestalt, we learned to be therapists and then also have someone work with us. So you find out a lot of stuff that you don't know. We had feedback whether we wanted it or not. It started out to me feeling very critical and I know why that is and *why* I took it that way."

Somewhere during the process, the criticism that Cathy used to dread turned into something she looked forward to. She saw the value of other people's perceptions of her and how an outside observation could offer a different sort of clarity that she could not have achieved alone. She said she remembered thinking, "I can't wait to hear the feedback on this. What are the areas I need to work on? How am I perceived by others? And that kind of feedback was really helpful to me. I resisted that initially. I almost didn't do the second year of Gestalt. The second year of Gestalt was probably more powerful for me than the first."

Cathy said the program was so small that each class became like a family. The class ahead of hers acted as her class's mentors. Once Cathy entered her second year, she too became a mentor. She described the feeling as akin to having children, parents, and grandparents, all there to support one another. It was through these relationships and this process that Cathy, who had always felt like an individual and outsider, began to see herself as part of a family. Not just the Gestalt family that was created during her master's, but part of her birth family. Growing up, Cathy said she didn't feel that her mother was supportive of her in the way she needed her to be. Nor did she feel connected to her grandmother's heritage. That caused Cathy to feel isolated for many years. That all changed during one particularly powerful day of Gestalt practice. Cathy said, "We did an exercise where someone was behind me as if she were my mother. There was someone in front of me as if I were her mother so we had a whole generational line, and we put our hands on each other's shoulders and it was amazing—the actual feeling that I felt come through me. We all felt it. You know, I can feel the goose bumps now thinking about it. It was a shared experience and I just felt all the ancestors of my life come through me, and now I'm going to get tearful because it was so wonderful."

That moment, said Cathy, led her to understand her mother in a way she hadn't previously. And like the countless others Cathy had helped throughout her life, she felt compassion for her. She saw how her mother's anxiety prompted her to keep her children close and protected rather than letting them go out into the world. That one exercise not only helped her better understand her mother's motivations, but also gave Cathy a newfound connection to her ancestors, which in turn led to an even better relationship with her own children. She recalled, "At that moment I felt I could give so much to my daughter and my son. I just felt the ancestry coming through me, such love that I never allowed before, and it changed me. That changed me. I felt like I came from somewhere. I wasn't just alone."

Another thing that Cathy learned about herself while in the program was how her relationship with school had changed over time. Thinking back on that seventeen-year-old girl who thought she would fail if she went to college but who, decades later, graduated cum laude, she said she was able to feel proud of her accomplishments. And even more important, she felt proud of how she performed during her primary school experience, something she hadn't allowed herself to feel before. She told me she thought to herself, "When you started school so early, you graduated early. You made it. I mean, I certainly wasn't straight As. I struggled through it all, but I did it. That's when I realized, *I'm amazing!* I was able to pat myself on the back, something up until that point I was never able to do."

What Cathy learned about herself during her graduate school experience changed her life. On the outside, with or without those revelations, she was a married woman in her forties pursuing a degree. But inside, she had transformed. She had rid herself of old insecurities, changed the way she felt about her family, and gained the ability to open up to others and accept feedback in a way she never had done before. Cathy blossomed. And with that transformation, she didn't just improve her own life. She also gained the necessary skills to help others—after nearly two decades of work, she finally became a therapist.

Now that Cathy has been working as a marriage and family therapist for ten years, I asked her, "What's it like to live the dream? How does it feel to have gone through so much to finally be able to do

Jonathan Shedler, from the University of Colorado Denver School of Medicine, reviewed the empirical evidence for psychotherapy and found substantial support from over the years for this type of therapy.[5] In particular, Shedler found that patients who receive psychodynamic therapy "not only maintain therapeutic gains but also continue to improve over time."

Cathy has certainly followed that trajectory, learning through the process of therapy and then improving with the new tools she learned. As she said about her first experience with a therapist, having a safe place to talk just about herself was a powerful feeling, and one that allowed her to really work on her own issues.

professionally what you, in a way, have always wanted to do?" She told me, "For me personally, I feel good. It feels right for me. When people share their stories with me, I'm able to sit with other people's pain. You know, I don't get sucked into it. So I'm able to be there with them and they're so appreciative to have someone to be able to share something really painful with, who can witness it and not fall apart with you. Because they need someone they can lean on for that time or someone who can hear what they have to say. I feel that's a gift of mine. I'm a good listener and I care. And I'm strong enough to handle what it is that they're saying to me."

As with any job, even a dream job, Cathy has had to make adjustments to her life in order to take care of herself. Being present while people share their love, their pain, and everything in between can weigh a person down unless they find a way to purge the pain of others. Cathy has implemented a variety of strategies to make sure that her life is balanced and that she is as well taken care of as her clients. She told me, "Therapists sometimes need to flush what they hear also, so I learned about that and I've paid attention and kept things in my life, daily things that I do that fill me up."

I asked Cathy what those things were—the people, places, and small details that keep her healthy and whole. She started with the simple way she begins her day. Each night she sleeps well in a heated waterbed. Upon waking, she and Michael spend quiet time alone together. Cathy said, "Cuddling with my husband, I mean, that starts my day. Having his leg over mine or his arm over me; that is a great thing for me." Feeling well rested and already bonded with Michael, Cathy then goes into the kitchen to make herself a cappuccino. Her day starts out feeling great because she has all of that. It may seem small. A warm bed, a good beverage, and a snuggle with her partner. These are a part of a routine that allows Cathy to have time to herself before any demands are made upon her. As she goes through her morning rituals, she takes a moment to acknowledge what is happening. She said she pauses to feel gratitude. Sometimes she expresses appreciative thoughts internally, and sometimes she says them out loud. In addition to her appreciation for those simple comforts in her life, her gratitude also extends to her loved ones. To make sure they know how she feels, Cathy often writes notes or calls her friends and family to tell them they are cherished, to tell them she is grateful to have them in her life.

That thankfulness is of the utmost importance to Cathy. If something good comes to her, she doesn't take it for granted. She values it because she knows that she's lucky to have it. That's the power of gratitude. It enables us to look at our lives, even when things aren't going according to plan, and to feel good about what we *do* have rather than focusing on the things we don't have.

In studies on gratitude, researcher Robert Emmons has found that keeping a gratitude journal and engaging in other practices that involve showing appreciation help us mentally and physically. He notes that gratitude can build stronger immune systems, lower blood pressure, allow us to sleep better, and bring about more positive emotions and a more optimistic outlook. It can also help make people more compassionate, helpful, and forgiving and make them feel less lonely and/or isolated.[6]

Gratitude helps us feel connected to something bigger than ourselves. Rather than feeling like the world owes us something, we are able to feel thankful for even the little things, like a warm bath, a kind word from a stranger, or a good meal. Even just having a roof over our heads and clean water to drink when so many others are struggling for those basic necessities can inspire gratitude. When we look at our life through the lens of gratitude, we are able to handle the bad things better because we know we have good to use as a counterbalance.

In addition to those private rituals, Cathy makes sure to devote time each week to her marriage and friendships. She and Michael belong to a monthly concert series that they both enjoy. On Mondays and Thursdays, she and three friends get together to catch up and work out. Even though Cathy's sciatic nerve had been acting up during the time of the interview, that didn't stop her from seeing her friends and adjusting her workout so she could keep her routines intact. Twice a week she also has lunch with other friends. And regularly, Cathy talks on the phone with her children, now grown and living far from home, and her sisters. She also belongs to a monthly book club that keeps her reading and provides an opportunity to talk to others.

What I love about Cathy's relationships and the way she maintains them is that she has a regular schedule. She doesn't have to carve out thirty minutes or an hour in her busy day in order to spend time with the people she loves. The time is already set aside. As we get older and more commitments attempt to take over our lives (at least it feels that way to me), it can become more difficult to see friends. Those days of calling someone up and saying, "Brunch in an hour?" often seem to end when we're about twenty-five years old. By then, many people have boyfriends, girlfriends, spouses, children, double shifts, ailing parents, appointments, and any/every other kind of reason that they can't get together until three Saturdays from next Tuesday. The scheduling alone can become a roadblock to socializing. Because Cathy has standing dates that don't require ten emails going back and forth, very little planning is involved. She gets to see her friends and know that she has social time to look forward to without any of the frustration of complex planning. She also schedules time just for herself. That includes meditating either to prerecorded guided meditations or just sitting in silence by herself.

As I've gotten older, I've noticed that I was getting worse and worse at prioritizing the things I enjoy. I was more focused on productivity than seeing friends, working out, or meditating—those very practices that, as Cathy put it, fill her up. I know a lot of my friends have the same issues. Where friendships used to be a necessity, they instead get viewed as a luxury. And luxuries are the first to go when life gets busy. It should be exactly the opposite. I always feel cleansed when I come home from spending time with a friend. Same with a workout at the gym. I feel energized, renewed, and my mood is better. Even if I leave the house in a bad mood, perhaps anxious or sullen, I'll almost always come home from exercising free of those bad feelings. Fortunately, we can all fill ourselves up in these ways. All it takes is making the things we know we enjoy a priority rather than an afterthought.

On top of friendships, book clubs, concerts, and other fun activities, Cathy has also altered how she monitors media to protect herself from negativity. As I mentioned earlier, she said that at times she feels the need to flush what she hears at work. The very nature of her job is to listen and contemplate other people's problems. Sometimes these problems are small and sometimes they are massive. If she came home and turned on the news, what would she see? Murder, war, sexual violence, environmental catastrophe, cruelty . . . The list goes on. (And on. And on.) So for the past three years, Cathy has cut down on the amount of news she exposes herself to. She told me, "I really limit the news that I watch now and I really limit what I read because it's so saturated with negativity and the horrible stuff in the world that you don't get to see how many wonderful things are happening. I mean if you balance it out, there is so much more good and we're not seeing that part on a regular basis." Cathy didn't start limiting her media consumption until she began working as a therapist. I asked her if she thought she would have been able to handle more news before she entered into her profession and she said yes, that was probably true. Cathy's not saying that being an educated citizen isn't important, especially when it comes to world issues. Instead, she's asking why we don't hear as many stories about the wonderful and inspiring things that people do each day to help one another.

Along that same line, Cathy is also selective about her down time. She has come to a place where she understands that just because her phone rings doesn't mean she has to answer it. She told me, "I realize how much power I have, and I'm not giving it away." By choosing not to answer the phone, and by knowing that her voicemail is there and she can always call back, Cathy is prioritizing her own time and well-being over always catering to other people's needs. In an age where you can call someone's land line, then their cell, text them, e-mail them, and instant chat them—all in about two minute's time—it's vital that we give ourselves the space to know we don't have to respond to every inquiry that comes our way. If I wrote back to every email as it came in, I'd never leave my computer. Cathy is right. She does have the power, and by being selective, she is exercising it; she is protecting those quiet moments that allow her to recharge.

CATHY AND I TALKED AT GREAT LENGTH about her marriage of thirty-eight years. I was very interested in how Michael felt about her spending so many years pursuing her bachelor's and master's degrees to become a therapist. Turns out, it was never an issue. Michael lives by the philosophy "A happy wife is a happy life." Cathy explained, "Me being in school made me happy; therefore, he was making me happy by supporting what I did." It doesn't go just one way, him supporting her. They both want what's best for the other and don't stand in each other's way when one pursues an interest.

I think one of the best qualities of their marriage, stemming from the desire to ensure each other's happiness, is that they have a strong partnered life as well as a strong independent life. They are confident enough in their relationship to come together and separate depending on the activity. Cathy explained, "We have some similar interests and then we have some that are not. But we are accepting of that with each other, so he does his thing and I can do my thing. And that's okay. Sometimes they'll overlap or he'll do some things even though it's not what he wants to do, and I'll do some things that he wants to do that are not really what I would do. We're respectful of each other." It follows that each would support the other in pursuits such as school or hobbies.

They also have great communication. When I first met Michael (he's the one who originally pointed me toward Cathy when I mentioned my book), he told me that he and Cathy, in all their years together, have probably fought fewer than five times. They choose to find solutions instead of accusing and insulting the other person. Cathy has learned over the years not to hold on to anger. Many of us allow hurt feelings to gather over time, and then finally release them when one small issue pushes us over the top. As a simple example, imagine that your partner leaves his or her socks on the floor each day. He or she has been doing it for months, and every morning you pick the socks up and put them in the hamper. Finally one day, after one pair of socks too many, you unleash, telling your partner how frustrating and awful it is to have to pick up these dirty socks. What could have been resolved during the first week of socks being left on the floor has now escalated into an all-out fight. That's a simple (and a bit of a silly) example, but it's one I think we can all relate to. We often hold something small inside until it becomes something big, and then we explode.

Cathy described how she handles a problem: "I've learned so much more to live in the present moment because that's really where the power is. That's where you can react to something, that's the time to react to something in that situation. So things don't pile up for me the way they used to. I acknowledge that I'm stressed and I try to keep that to the issue that I'm stressed about, not pile anything else on, not add anything more. I'll vocalize if I am upset." She also never uses cheap shots. Over the years Michael and Cathy have discovered the other's hot buttons. Neither of them uses those while in an argument. They don't seek to hurt one another, just to solve the problem at hand.

Cathy told me, "I think I'm just a solution person in a way, and I don't want to jump the gun and I don't want to make something bigger than what it is. That came directly from my childhood. My mother could rage at something so I've learned not to do that. Get your facts first and then move forward." While her mother would show her anger, her father set a different example. She said, "My

In three studies looking at social relationships in a group of 544 college students in Germany, Spain, and the United States, researchers found that those who displayed higher levels of emotional intelligence—the ability to recognize and regulate one's emotions—were better able to manage conflicts with others, giving them stronger social relationships and enabling them to resolve conflicts and bond with others.[7] Cathy's desire to stay "coolheaded" and not let situations get bigger than they are shows that she is able to understand her emotional state and not let it negatively impact her relationships.

father was more coolheaded; he'd get the information and then act, so I kind of saw that as well. That appealed to me more, so I worked more toward that and I still do that in my everyday life."

This one trait, to work toward solutions and to have conversations rather than arguments, enables people to stay calm, not overreact and say things they end up regretting. They aren't seeking to win an argument or a discussion. They want to find the best resolution possible. It means knowing that we are not and cannot always be right—it's statistically impossible. Having the flexibility to change one's attitude or plans and to see another person's point of view is a characteristic that can work to one's benefit in a marriage, in the workplace, and within a friendship. Heck, it can even work while on the phone with customer service representatives. Cathy gave insight into how she and Michael handle two different viewpoints by explaining, "This is how you feel. This is how I feel. This is what we want to do. How are we going to get there? What compromises are we going to make, if any? Are we going to agree to disagree at this point?"

Above all else, what contributes to their happy marriage, and this should go without saying, is that Cathy and Michael still love each other. They are not only romantic partners but also great friends. In all their years together, Cathy doesn't believe a day has gone by when they haven't spoken to each other. Even when they are apart, they check in by phone. Flexibility and understanding are the tools to make a relationship thrive, but none of it would matter if there wasn't first love and the genuine desire to be with someone. Michael and Cathy have that—in spades.

I TOOK SO MUCH AWAY from my time with Cathy. She exemplifies the numerous characteristics I was searching for: perseverance, growth, patience, kindness, and the courage to pursue dreams even when they are difficult. To figure out your passion in your late twenties, and then take the long road to gain two degrees, all to become a therapist two decades later, takes some doing. During the time she was in school, she was still able to savor those magical moments with her kids. It was a long, slow road, but it was the only road she wanted to take. Yes, Cathy has a lot to teach us about what it means to choose the life we want, to continue to grow as a person, and how important it is to keep our childhood passions alive within us. I think young Cathy McInerney would be thrilled by the life she now leads. She was born to be a therapist and, as luck would have it, the process of becoming that therapist healed many of her wounds from the past. I'll raise my glass to that.

BUILDING A RICH
AND MEANINGFUL LIFE
AFTER A TRAUMA

·

*How can someone who has experienced
the worst horrors imaginable go on to live
a peaceful, hopeful, and happy life?*

"To go on you have to make an attempt to separate the
future from the past, and for some time along the way
I pretended *I'm not the person who went through all that.
That's someone else.* I had to make an enormous attempt
to concentrate on the present and the future, not be,
emotionally, a prisoner of the past."

—Emery Jacoby

chapter 3

Emery,

Holocaust Survivor and Compassionate Optimist

IF YOU EVER HAVE THE GOOD FORTUNE to meet Emery Jacoby, there are two things you can be sure of. The first is that you will have the privilege of being hugged and kissed by one of the kindest men you'll ever meet. (He hugs and kisses everyone.) The second is that when you say good-bye, you'll already be looking forward to the next time you will see him.

Emery, born in Romania in 1924, is now ninety years old, has been married for more than sixty years, and is confident he'll be around for many more. His love for his wife, his family, his friends, and his immense sense of compassion for the world around him are contagious. Perhaps that's why I was so struck by his story. It's not just that he's a man who is at peace with himself; it's that he's at peace despite experiencing one of the most horrific events in history and examples of human cruelty one can imagine. In addition to being an architect, a designer, a world traveler, a husband, a father, and a grandfather, Emery is a Holocaust survivor. He's living proof that no matter how devastating the trauma, a person can go on to live a powerful, safe, and fulfilling life.

As a young man growing up in Tirgu Mures, Romania, Emery already knew that he wanted to leave his country. Corruption and anti-Semitism were commonplace, and life, as Emery put it, "was a struggle." He told me, "My dream was always that I would get someplace where there was an opportunity for a better life." Of course, those dreams had to be put on hold with the outbreak of World War II.

On April 17, 1944, at twenty years old, Emery Jacoby was taken by the Nazis, along with the other fifteen- to twenty-five-year-old Jewish men in his town. For the next six months, he and thousands of others were led on a forced death march for hundreds of miles through Hungary to the Austrian border.

He and the other men were fed rotten cabbage soup, made to carry rocks and dig trenches, and slept however and wherever they could along the side of the road. For half a year, despite being hungry, tired, and exposed to the elements, Emery kept going, putting one foot in front of the other while all around him boys and men, his friends and neighbors, were dying from lack of food, exhaustion, and executions. Emery estimates that around 70 percent of his companions perished on that march. He told me with a hint of sadness, "Luckily, I was in very good shape, healthy. I survived." Even though their long walk was over, those who endured were brought to a new nightmare. They entered Dachau, a concentration camp northwest of Munich to face more torture, humiliation, and murder.

In many ways, I think Emery's personality, one that is infused with an unflinching sense of hope, is what got him through the war. That and, of course, some good luck. Just days after arriving at Dachau, Emery said Munich "was bombed to oblivion and many of the major buildings collapsed." The bombing was so severe that Germany didn't have enough workers to rescue the people who were trapped beneath the rubble. Because Dachau was so close, any reasonably fit prisoners from the camp were trucked into Munich to work. That was Emery's good fortune. A Hungarian train carrying soldiers on recreation was nearby. He was able to get hold of an extra pair of pants and a shirt, pose as a Hungarian soldier, and, remarkably, walk away.

He had escaped the concentration camp, a feat all by itself, but danger was still everywhere in Europe, and Emery was hundreds of miles from home. Drawing on his ability to speak multiple languages and to blend into his surroundings, Emery managed to travel all the way to the city of Graz in Austria where he hid among the enemy, working as an auto mechanic, hoping he wouldn't be discovered by the Nazi soldiers who were working day and night to exterminate an entire population of people. His people.

When the Russians eventually came, it meant freedom for many.

However, Emery had been hiding in plain sight and knew he wouldn't be recognized as one of the oppressed. He fled on a motorcycle and hid in a barn, but was captured days later. He found himself inside a Russian prison camp. Yes, another prison.

With the help of two partisans, Jewish freedom fighters, his time there was short. Together, they slipped under the barbed wire as his companions bargained and bribed their way free. Had he not been helped, he would have soon found himself on the way to Siberia with the other prisoners.

AFTER A LONG YEAR OF IMPRISONMENT, mental and physical torture, and hiding, Emery was a free man but still far from home. He had no idea if his mother, father, and two sisters were dead or alive. Like many other displaced people, Emery began his long journey home through a chaotic Europe. When he did eventually find his way back to Tirgu Mures, he was reunited with his sisters, but the reunion was bittersweet. They told him that their mother and father had perished at Auschwitz. Days after Emery was taken, his remaining family was brought to the concentration camp where they, too, experienced unimaginable suffering. His sisters were freed the day before they were scheduled to be sent to the crematorium. One more day and Emery would have been the sole survivor of his immediate family.

UPON HEARING EMERY'S STORY, a few questions kept repeating themselves in my head. What was it that kept him going? Not just during the Holocaust, but after. How does someone go back to any kind of normal life, let alone flourish the way he has, after seeing the very worst of what humanity is capable of?

It's been about seventy years since Emery was taken from his home. Sitting in the same room as us was his wife of sixty years, Elaine, and his grandson, Sam, who at the time of the interview was twenty years old, the same age Emery was when he became a prisoner. I looked at the two of them and wondered how anyone so young, so innocent, could survive such brutality.

"Seventy percent of the people on that march didn't make it. What do you think you had inside you that helped you survive?" I asked Emery. This was a tough question, and he needed a second to gather himself before responding. He had told me before the interview that as he's gotten older, he's gotten more emotional. So when he answered, it was with a quivering voice. He said, "I was convinced that I wasn't going to die. And it worked." He explained, "The minute you gave up it was practically over. Because, there was no food, no clothing; you were exposed to the elements, the hopelessness. You had to be a moron to think you were going to survive. Everyone was being killed all around you. Why should you be the exception?"

And yet, Emery believed he would live. He pushed forward, showing the true meaning of the word "resilience." He could have given in to the exhaustion during the march across Hungary and Austria. He could have lost his will to fight. This man had experienced hundreds, if not thousands, of moments when giving up would have been easier than fighting for life. But Emery is not a person who gives up. He's a born optimist, a trait that probably saved his life during the war.

As part of his research on resilience, Dr. Dennis Charney, dean of Mount Sinai School of Medicine, examined the lives of 750 Vietnam War veterans, largely pilots, who had been prisoners of war for between six and eight years.[8] Despite being tortured and/or kept in solitary confinement, these men did not develop depression or post-traumatic stress disorder (PTSD). When looking at this population of people who had suffered extreme stress and trauma, he discovered they shared many qualities. The top three included optimism, altruism, and having a moral compass. Emery, who was also tortured and imprisoned, although he was not in the armed forces at the time, is, in my opinion, a master at all three of those valued traits. He believed he would live despite overwhelming evidence to the contrary; he showed kindness toward others even when it could bring him personal harm. He also had and has a solid moral compass, one that also gives his life a greater meaning (another item on the list of qualities those men shared). Emery has shown that resilience and optimism can get a person through even the most difficult circumstances and continue to aid that person once their life has normalized.

Survival is one thing. Living with the memories of what he endured was a completely different obstacle. The first step in this task for Emery when he returned home was to create some distance between the nightmare he had lived through and his new life. Thousands from his immediate community had perished in concentration camps, and many who had survived were traumatized. He had friends who had lived through the Holocaust only to take their own lives once the war ended. Living with the memories and the loss of loved ones was too much. That's why Emery separated himself from the experience. He told me, "I realized the magnitude of the tragedy—that most of my friends in the city where we lived, that large parts of the population were exterminated." He paused before continuing, "To go on, you have to make an attempt to separate the future from the past, and for some time along the way I pretended *I'm not the person who went through all that. That's someone else.* I had to make an enormous attempt to concentrate on the present and the future, not be, emotionally, a prisoner of the past."

In order to survive, Emery had become a master at pretending to be someone else, which in a strange way prepared him for this next stage of life after the war. With great mental strength and determination, he was able to create the emotional distance necessary to move on with his life. Detaching from the man who had survived the Holocaust allowed him to make sure his sisters were married and cared for so he could travel across Europe to finally pursue his dream. He got out of Romania and traveled to the United States as a refugee to start a new life.

But even now, while he relays the timeline and events that happened on the march, at Dachau, and in the Russian prison camp, Emery doesn't talk about the specific horrors he witnessed. Reliving those moments over and over is a rabbit hole Emery won't let himself go down. He likes to, as he says, "focus on the positive."

He witnessed how many other survivors become stuck in their memories. After the war, some wouldn't leave their homes. Some had lost everyone they knew before the war. The Holocaust was over, but still, they were not safe. In their minds, they were still inside those camps.

Emery didn't keep his emotional distance forever. He told me, "Later on when I got settled here in America, then I resumed my old self and admitted what had happened."

Creating space between himself and the Holocaust was Emery's first coping mechanism. It was a quick bandage placed on a gaping wound to staunch the bleeding and keep him moving forward. But real healing? That came later. It all started with the belief that with a positive attitude, the kind of life he wanted to live was in reach, no matter what he had endured in his past.

I think of others who have experienced enormous suffering reading his story and realizing that it's possible not only to survive great trauma but to flourish afterward. I wish everyone could spend an hour with Emery, so they could see living proof that no matter what we experience, there is a way to move forward. Our past is always a part of us, but our present and future, that's forever ours to mold. And Emery did just that.

After hearing about Emery's time during the war and his immediate coping mechanisms, we dug deeper into what he chose to do after moving to America. It was not the big events in his life that changed him but how he chose (and still chooses) to interact with people and the greater world. Whether it's exercising great self-control, learning to be a flexible and considerate spouse, or working out to keep his body healthy, Emery had words of wisdom that can help us all lead a good life.

AS I SAID, THE HOLOCAUST was *a* defining moment in Emery's life, not *the* defining moment. After arriving in the United States in 1948, Emery's life took a vastly different turn. He was called upon by the U.S. government to join the Army, and so he did. Emery joked that during his time in the Army, he advanced farther than Hitler had. He said with a smile, "I'm better than Hitler." I responded, "I think we can all agree that that's true." He joined the Army swim team and traveled all around the States competing against other teams. Emery left the service to pursue his education and study architecture in Brooklyn.

It wasn't his time in the Army, his education, or his career that gave him the biggest gift in his life. That came when Emery was set up on a blind date with a young woman named Elaine. He was working at a large architectural firm in New York when a doctor from his hometown immigrated to the United States. The doctor was having a difficult time starting his practice, so another immigrant, Elaine's father, decided to help him get settled, as he did for many other refugees. As Emery tells it, the doctor said to Elaine's father, "I understand you have a daughter. I know a young man who has just arrived. Could I introduce him to your daughter?" Emery met Elaine at her home on Fifth Avenue. On the end of their very first date, she told her mother, "I've never met anyone like him in my life, and I would marry him tomorrow."

Elaine and Emery have enjoyed what Emery calls a sixty-year honeymoon. He's not poking fun. He really means it. Together, the couple built a family, now with children and grandchildren, as well as an intricate network of friends. For Emery, marriage and relationships became the cornerstone of his new charmed life.

A great marriage doesn't magically appear. There is something special about Emery and Elaine that has allowed them to forever remain on this glorious honeymoon. Their marriage has stayed strong not just because of their mutual love (which is immense), but because, much like Cathy and Michael, they are both able to regulate their emotions. Emery may have witnessed the kind of cruelty most people can't even imagine. He managed to thrive in spite of it. Unlike those who react to the world with anger, jealousy, and hatred, Emery seems to have only love.

He told me, "I swear to you in sixty years I never raised my voice. Ever. Never apologized, never had to." How did he manage such an incredible feat?

He said, "Number one, unquestionable love. The next most important thing is tolerance. You have to be tolerant. Two people growing up in different environments, in different worlds, have differences of opinion. You have to have enormous mutual respect."

When I first heard those words, I thought only about his relationship with Elaine, how his marriage is filled with understanding and compassion for his wife. Then it occurred to me that his philosophy on marriage applies to all of his other relationships as well. Emery has an even temperedness about him that allows him to hear others instead of reacting defensively. He compromises; he discusses and looks for common ground.

I got the impression that Emery is kind to the core and, perhaps even more important, has the discipline of mind to not let the small

Leslie C. Burpee and Ellen J. Langer, in their study "Mindfulness and Marital Satisfaction," found that having the knack for discussing a problem and working to see the other's point of view is perhaps the single most important signifier of a happy marriage.[9] This is the skill that Emery and Elaine appear to have mastered in their six-decade marriage. Burpee and Langer write, "Drawing distinctions across situations, acknowledging the existence of alternative perspectives and recognizing disadvantages may also be advantages from others' points of view, may help foster more positive and satisfying relationships by creating an environment that is rich with open-mindedness and flexibility, rather than criticism and rigidity."

stuff bother him. He described how he resolves conflicts with his words, the most powerful tool one has in any sort of relationship, and one I can personally attest to. I'll be the first to admit that, although I'm on the path to finding a balanced and satisfying life, not all of the pieces are in place yet. But a happy marriage? That's something I have in common with Emery. I told him that in more than seven years of marriage (a fraction of his), Gary and I have also never yelled. We've learned that talking builds stronger relationships. Emery and Elaine are living proof of that.

The old cliché is true. You have to give a little to get a little. As I said, a sixty-year honeymoon doesn't just happen without work and a whole lot of mental discipline. People who talk through their difficulties rather than yell aren't necessarily less prone to negative emotions than others. It's just that they recognize that conversation works to improve even the most delicate of situations, while yelling, passive aggressiveness, or retaliation only increases the divide between two people. If we all treat every problem as something we want to resolve and work to see things from the other person's perspective, conflict resolution becomes a collaborative process.

Compromise and respect and the ability to live in the present moment aren't the only things that have kept Emery and Elaine going strong all these years. Remember when I mentioned that if you met Emery, he'd most likely kiss you on the cheek and give you a hug? The simple act of touching our partners can make a huge difference in the quality of our relationships.

People in a happy marriage can enjoy all sorts of benefits. Studies have shown that happily married couples are less prone to dementia, pneumonia, cancer, depression, heart attacks, and other medical misfortunes. For those who have faced life-threatening illnesses, some research shows that people with a spouse are likely to do better in the recovery process than those without.[10]

When Emery and Elaine walk down the street, he said they hold hands. They kiss, smile at each other, and sit side by side. Elaine chimed in on the conversation at this point and commented about how people react to their public displays of affection, "We always hold hands, and now that we're not so young, people say, 'oh, how cute.'"

Why cute? Sadly, in many relationships the amount of touching decreases the longer the couple has been together. Early in a courtship, holding hands might be the norm. Couples kiss hello and goodbye, or kiss for no other reason than they care about the person they are with. As we get older, more comfortable, and more engrossed in the day-to-day grind, nonsexual touch seems to become less of a priority. Ask yourself how many couples over forty do you see touching each other as they walk down the street? Emery and Elaine hold hands. They kiss. They cuddle. That's why strangers approach them. They touch because it's a way for them to express their love. Sixty years later, they continue to express their affection much like two people who are dating. And that helps keep their bond strong.

In a 2013 article in *Psychology Today*, author Rick Chillot discusses the importance of touch in all kinds of relationships.[11] When he examines marriage, he notes that new couples tend to do a lot of touching and that this continues to increase through the early part of a marriage. Perhaps that's what popular culture commonly refers to as the honeymoon phase. Sadly, as the marriage continues, nonsexual touching begins to taper off. People get used to each other. The sensation of touch perhaps no longer inspires the same butterflies and good feelings they did previously. But comfort, partnership, love? All of those emotions that are vital to a long and healthy marriage can be expressed nonverbally. All it takes is a reach of the hand.

Emery's relationships with his wife, children, and grandchildren aren't the only sources of happiness in his life. He's also developed a robust community of friends and neighbors who bring him immense joy.

As he describes them, his relationships aren't surface-level see-you-next-summer sorts of arrangements. He told me about one friendship that developed fifty-five years ago. Despite the other couple living in London, they still call each other every week and have been known to fly in for events and then fly back the next day. Emery says, "Another couple who lived in New Jersey had a farm and two children. We were house guests there every weekend for twenty years."

Emery explained that the way to make valuable friendships is to deserve the friendship of decent and honest people by being decent and honest ourselves. I understand this to mean that if we give ourselves fully to the relationships in our lives by helping others when they need assistance and by being true to our own values, we will find joy through the relationships we build just like Emery did. And as you'll see in this next story, he stayed true to his philosophy about friendship even when it came with great personal risk.

During the war when the Russians were approaching, the Germans moved Emery and the other prisoners west. He told me, "They asked who speaks fluent German. I volunteered. Every morning for about five or six days we had to line up and I had to go in front of an SS [a member of a major Nazi military organization under Hitler] and had to report in German how many people were present. He told me, 'If I count the seventy-five, if one is missing, you'll be the first one to be killed and ten others.' When he ordered us to march, one of my close friends couldn't get up. We slept on wooden boards about four stories high covered with hay. We covered him and I went outside and reported everybody present. And he was left in there and we marched away, and he went home the next day." The Germans left, bringing Emery and all the others except his friend on to Dachau. Most of the men died, but Emery's friend lived. The Russians came, and he went home.

Ten years later Emery saw this man in Israel, and this old friend told Elaine the story of Emery, the courageous man who saved his life. People usually don't know how brave they'll be until they are in the moment when their courage is tested. Emery had his moment, and he proved himself to be more than decent and honest. He was a hero. And, of course, an incredible friend.

Emery's story caused me to wonder if I have a friend who would do something like that for me. Could I do it for someone else? I like to think I would, but unlike Emery, I've never been tested. I do know that there are many ways that we can be heroes to our friends in our daily lives. Kind words help when a friend is struggling, and a listening ear can sometimes make all the difference. It is apparent that Emery lives by the golden rule: treat others the way you want to be treated. And because of that, he's surrounded by those who love him and who he loves equally in return.

It is common to think that we need to have a plethora of friends in order to lead a fulfilling life, which is why many people believe that extroverts have the most fun and the most satisfying relationships. (Emery certainly is an extrovert.) If you're an introvert like me, have no fear. We don't need to be out partying every night or have thirty close friends who we brunch with every weekend to fill our friendship quota. Having a handful of close friends, ones we love so much we would drive them to the airport on short notice, accompany them to the doctor, or accept the "there's a strange noise outside my house" calls from at 4:00 a.m., will do quite nicely.

THERE WERE MANY QUALITIES that Emery possesses that I found myself vowing to work on as soon as I exited his New York City apartment, like making more time to nurture the friendships in my life and even creating a few new ones. But it was when Emery started talking about how he handles anxiety and worrying, nearly repeating word for word what Sungrai had told me, that I knew I had stumbled upon something really special that I wanted to strive to achieve.

As strange as it sounds to someone like me and to the vast majority of chronic worrywarts I know, Emery Jacoby doesn't get stressed. He doesn't wake up at 2:00 a.m. fixating on a problem, rolling it over in his mind a hundred times as his heart rate increases and his palms begin to sweat. Instead, the man sees a problem and if he can help fix it, he tackles it head-on. No sleepless nights and no hoping for the best but preparing for the worst.

When I asked Emery how he handles stress, he told me, "I developed a marvelous solution to that problem. When a problem arises, no matter what it is, I have two questions: Can I do something about it or can't I? If I can do something about it, I call on my force; I do everything humanly possible to solve the problem. If I can't do something about it, I go to sleep. If I can't do anything about it, what's the sense of killing myself or destroying my disposition, not only my own but of everyone around me?"

Sound familiar? My jaw nearly dropped when Emery spoke those words. They were so similar to Sungrai's that I had to stop the interview and actually laugh, recalling the advice Dorothy DeLay gave to Sungrai: "Why worry? Instead of wasting time worrying, do something about it."

Sungrai and Emery are two men with nearly thirty years between them, born on two different continents, and yet, somehow, they both reached the same conclusion when it comes to combating anxiety. I started writing this book to find out not just what one satisfied person does and feels, but to explore the many things such people have in common. If one person gives me advice, it's an idea to consider. If multiple people who are successful in one particular area start doling out the same wisdom, it's definitely time to take notice.

I won't spend much time going into Emery's solution to worrying, mostly because it would be déjà vu. I hope you take away from his advice the same thing I did. When a problem presents itself (and they always do), and we find ourselves sitting still and worrying, we should just stop. Stop that very second. As Emery told me, "It doesn't do any good." Instead, we can ask ourselves what we could do to make the problem better. At the end of the day, we can only control our own actions. Nothing else. Not the weather, not the behaviors of others. Only ourselves.

IN THE BEGINNING OF THIS BOOK, I said that the people I interviewed are active participants in their own stories. They know that they can't control every little problem that comes their way, but they do their best to change anything they can change. Or even better, they take action to prevent problems from happening in the first place. That also rings true for one of Emery's daily routines that I know many of us promise ourselves we'll do, but sometimes can't quite muster the energy to accomplish. We all have daily rituals. Maybe it's a cup of coffee or a ten-minute meditation. For him, it's waking up his body with a rigorous workout. Emery goes to the gym every morning at 5:00 a.m. I think this also speaks to something I touched on earlier. Discipline.

Sungrai is disciplined. So is Emery. He's not a person who says, "I'll work out tomorrow." When I asked him why he works out every morning, he said, "Because I am aware that there are only two things you can do in life: what you do with your body and what you put in your mouth. I don't put anything in my body that's not right. I don't eat much meat and I don't drink anything that does harm to this beautiful body," he said with a hearty chuckle. "Of course, exercise keeps me young and vibrant mentally."

Emery is one of the most active people I know. I add no qualifiers to that like *Emery is one of the most active ninety-year-olds I know.* He's one of the most active people I've ever met, age be damned. He believes in diet and exercise as a vital portion of his day because it serves as preventative medicine.

When I originally called Emery to set up our interview, I left a voicemail. Three days later when I hadn't heard back from him, I started to worry. I mean, the man is ninety. Turns out, worrying was silly (and perhaps a little ageist). When he phoned me back about four or five days later, he apologized for the delay and told me he and his wife had been driving through the mountains in Virginia. How many ninety-year-olds do you know who take those kinds of holidays? He has stayed young because he cares for his body and his mind. This allows him to continue to enjoy a high quality of life and to remain in his home and drive through the mountains for a romantic long weekend with Elaine.

I've played sports ever since my parents signed me up for T-ball when I was a little girl. That led to horseback riding, basketball, softball, and volleyball. As I got older and it became harder to wrangle my peers to join in a pickup game, and when I began to have severe disabling pain in my feet, I started lifting weights, doing abdominal exercises, and trying to find any way to keep active, despite my limitations. Part of it is because I know working out is good for me physically. The bigger part is that I know that there are two main reasons my mood starts to drop: (1) I'm not writing and (2) I'm not working

Researchers from the University of Western Australia recruited 12,000 Australian men between the ages of sixty-five and eighty-three for what they called
the "Health in Men Study." They followed these men for thirteen years, studying
how being active affects one's health as they age. The results showed that men
who were active were less prone to depression, memory loss, and functional
incapacity. Lead author of the study, Osvaldo Almeida, said about the results,
"So not only were active people more likely than non-active people to survive,
but those who were alive and active when we followed up had reached old age
in good shape, without evidence of depression or of cognitive or functional
problems. In other words they were able to move about and do their business without significant assistance—looking after their finances, looking after
themselves, looking after their house, etc., and they did not have any evidence
of mental illness."[12]

out. On days when I do both, it's like someone gave me a happy pill. I
know I've worked my body and mind. Everything after that is a bonus.

I don't know if Emery's past inspired him to take the best possible
care of his body or if that's something he would have done regardless.
I do know that a near-death experience, an illness, or any big life
change that happens can lead us to appreciate our physical form in
ways we never have before. After I was diagnosed with cancer, the
first thing I did was go for a run. A few weeks before my surgery, I
climbed Sleeping Giant in Connecticut, a beautiful hike up a small
mountain. Emery is fully present mentally and physically. He knows
that his physical health is related to his mental health. As I said, I
don't know if the Holocaust prompted him to become so vigilant
about taking care of himself. I do know that it has helped him continue to live a good life even as he has aged. There aren't too many
men who still live in their own homes at ninety years old or who
work out every morning. I only hope that I'll have the strength to do
the same one day.

EMERY HAS TRULY GONE ON TO LIVE the positive life he hoped for
when he left Romania all those years ago. But, even when we are
able to thrive after a trauma, our experience never truly leaves us. In
addition to living a meaningful life through his family, friends, and

work, Emery has made advocating for a peaceful world his mission. While it's difficult to talk about the Holocaust, he said he knows that the best way to ensure it never happens again is to educate others.

Although the Holocaust ended in 1945, the root causes for the genocide, like hatred and bigotry, have never disappeared. We see them in milder forms each and every day when we witness hate crimes, bullying, racism, anti-Semitism, homophobia, Islamophobia, and sexism, to name a few. Around the world genocides have happened since the Holocaust, and tragically, they will continue. Emery recognizes that humanity is flawed and knows intimately how quickly the hate that infects society can lead to something far more sinister. In the case of the Holocaust, an estimated six million Jews lost their lives. That piece of knowledge—that the world can turn against you so quickly because of what you believe or what you look like—is hard to live with. For Emery, that knowledge has also given him a sense of purpose in life. He lives by the words of the famous writer Elie Wiesel (another Holocaust survivor), "To listen to a witness is to become one." And so, Emery tells others about the Holocaust. He talks about it to anyone who will listen.

In a 2010 speech in Newark, New Jersey, on Holocaust Remembrance Day, Emery told a group of schoolchildren, "As you well know, history repeats itself. All you have to do is read the most incredible stories about Kosovo, Rwanda, Bosnia, Nigeria, the Congo, and so many other countries where innocent people are slaughtered. It is your generation's responsibility to rebuke racism, anti-Semitism, hatred, discrimination." Emery also took on this topic in an AMA (Ask Me Anything) on Reddit (a social networking service). When asked if it's difficult for him to watch films on the Holocaust, he replied, "Yes, it is difficult, but I think it's important the story be told so people are aware of the evil man has the capability of committing. And while awareness is important, there is nothing more crucial than taking concrete action against bigotry and hatred no matter the race, religion, or group of people being targeted."

Educating others about his experience is, as Emery calls it, his "mission." He hopes that through technology, books, and films the stories of those with first-hand accounts of the Holocaust will live on. In fact, that's probably the biggest reason Emery said yes to taking part in this project. He told me that if one person reads his story in this book, it will have been worth it. Therefore, you, dear reader, have made it a success.

This sense of purpose is arguably part of the reason Emery has lived such a long and healthy life. The Rush Memory and Aging Project has shown that those who believe they have a higher purpose in life have a reduced risk of mortality, better cognition, and reduced risk of diseases like Alzheimer's. Patricia A. Boyle, one of the minds behind the Rush Memory and Aging Project, said, "The finding that purpose in life is related to longevity in older persons suggests that aspects of human flourishing—particularly the tendency to derive meaning from life's experiences and possess a sense of intentionality and goal-directedness—contribute to successful aging."[13]

The beautiful thing about purpose is that it always gives us a reason to get up in the morning. When we have purpose, our task is never quite complete so it always needs attention. It's a lifelong goal or way of living that we aspire to. Purpose doesn't look the same for everyone. For some, it might be to nurture their family; for others, their art. Many activists have given their lives to a cause outside of themselves.

Emery told me during the course of the interview, "Every individual has exactly the same right to pursue happiness and the kind of life he dreams about." Despite a tragic start in life, Emery has done exactly that. He has pursued the life of his dreams. He doesn't dwell on his past any more than he has to. When he talks about it, it's to educate others. Most of his time is spent with his wife, family, and friends, enjoying his years in retirement. To be in Emery's presence is to feel balanced. It's contagious! He focuses on the positive and shows enormous gratitude for the life he leads. A sixty-year marriage, children, a fulfilling career, hobbies, friends, and trips around the world—Emery has led an incredible life, proving that one's past doesn't have to determine one's future. Witnessing hate doesn't mean you have to internalize hate. Emery is one of the kindest people I've ever met, showing that human beings are resilient and capable of as much joy and beauty as they are of destruction. It's all about the paths we choose.

LIVING OUR VALUES

·

*How do activists remain positive and engaged
in the midst of suffering and despair?*

"Becoming a humane educator for me was the actual
solution to burnout, depression, despair, apathy—any of
those things—because I saw how powerful this work was.
I saw the change. It was heartening. It felt great. I felt
great. It's a win for me, it's a win for my students, and it's
a win for all of the people, animals, and the environment
whom they affect."

—Zoe Weil

chapter 4

Zoe,

*Cofounder of the Institute for Humane Education
and Dedicated "Solutionary"*

ONE OF MY OWN BIGGEST HURDLES in living a balanced life is the knowledge that suffering is all around me. People who are sick or starving, a planet that is being choked by pollution, animals who are tortured en masse for cheap food, women who are sold into the sex trade, children and the elderly who are dying because they don't have something as simple as clean water, genocide, racism, homophobia, speciesism, and countless other injustices are all taking place at this very second in every corner of the planet. This knowledge can be enough to stop a sensitive person's heart. That's why it was so important for me to find and talk to an activist—someone who truly feels compassion for others and the desire to help—who has found a way to live a balanced life, even in the face of all the horror.

Not too long after I began identifying subjects for my book, I heard Zoe Weil speak at a conference in New York City. Now fifty-two years old, Zoe has been working as a pioneer in a field known as humane education. She cofounded the Institute for Humane Education in 1996, an organization that trains and educates teachers on how to create a kinder world through teaching youth about human rights, animal protection, and environmental ethics. In Zoe's perfect world, children in every school would be taught to become "solutionaries." They'd learn about important global issues like child labor, endangered species, and pollution so they could start to imagine ways we can all work to fix those problems through our personal actions and through our collective efforts. To do this work and to do it well, Zoe has to be knowledgeable about all sorts of issues, from modern-day slavery to animal testing to climate change. It's a lot for the brain to digest. When I saw Zoe up on stage, I knew she would be a perfect person to interview. Even though she's constantly exposed to difficult topics, she remains joyful and full of enough energy to inspire others. I was especially excited to talk to her because humane education has been my area of activism for the past eight years. Working at an organization called HEART, a part of my job is to teach kids about human rights, animal protection, and environmental preservation in classrooms and after school clubs. It's a badge I wear proudly.

Zoe didn't grow up knowing that she would become an activist. She said she has always been very sensitive to any kind of injustice, and as a teenager was often inconsolable after being exposed to cruelty of any kind. That didn't stop her from watching films or reading books on important subjects. She described her experience with the television series *Roots* as a young woman and how, even though it was devastating, she continued watching it because she felt like it was her responsibility to be a witness, to be informed. (Emery would be proud.)

Even though Zoe had all of these strong emotions, no one in her family ever mentioned that activism was a path she could pursue. Zoe told me, "I did not grow up in a household in which I was taught that I either had the capacity or the responsibility to try to solve problems. I certainly *was* taught that I had capacity and responsibility to be successful, but that success meant being a doctor or being an astronaut or being a great business leader—but not being a change-maker. So change-making was not part of my mind-set or my vision for my future."

It took years for Zoe to figure out that activism, specifically in the form of humane education, was the path that would bring her the most satisfaction and joy in life. Throughout her college years and beyond Zoe studied for many potential professions. She was briefly pre-med; obtained her master's in English, thinking she would be a professor; received another master's from Harvard Divinity School, again believing that she wanted to be a professor; and even went to law school for a few months before dropping out. None of this was wasted effort. Zoe explained, "I love being in school. It almost doesn't matter what I'm studying." In addition to her studies, Zoe worked a variety of jobs ranging from a bookstore clerk to a naturalist. At the same time she tried her hand at various sorts of activism, like leafleting and protesting. While all of it was interesting, none of the avenues she tried ignited her passion enough to make her want to pursue it as her life's work. That all changed after she took a job teaching week-long summer courses to middle school children at the University of Pennsylvania.

Zoe describes that experience as her epiphany. She loved teaching, but helping kids understand English and theology wasn't enough for her. She ultimately had to partner the right skill with the right subject matter. She said about that summer program, "That's where I discovered there is a way to combine what I realized I was good at and liked doing, teaching, with what I really cared about, which were these social justice issues. I taught those courses; I watched those kids change. It was amazing."

How many people would have stopped at their master's in English and from there gone on to become an English teacher? Zoe's search for something that excited her went on far longer than for anyone I've ever met. I think somewhere along the way, many of us give up on the search for the perfect fit. It's like millions of people are walking around in shoes that are slightly too large or too small. Early on, Zoe found half of her puzzle, her love of teaching. Until she paired it with her passion for world issues, however, she wasn't finished. She didn't know exactly what she wanted. She knew herself well enough to realize that the areas she had explored wouldn't fulfill her. One could argue it was an expensive journey filled with multiple degrees from schools spanning from Boston to New York to Philadelphia to Washington, DC. I would say that her journey was instrumental in helping her know what she didn't want so she could finally recognize the perfect fit when she found it. It's the kissing-a-lot-of-frogs-to-find-a-prince philosophy.

It also speaks to a broader theme, something Zoe has in common with each of the people featured in this book: a passion for what she does for a living. Think of Sungrai, the violinist and teacher, and

Cathy, the family and marriage therapist. Both are passionate about their jobs. Most of us spend a minimum of forty hours per week dedicating our skills and education to working toward a particular task. That amounts to a lot of time per day, and a huge chunk of one's life. If that job bores us or goes against our ethics, or if the work environment is toxic, it can be difficult to stay balanced. I have certainly, out of necessity, worked jobs that didn't fulfill me. Unless born wealthy, we'd be hard pressed to find a person who hasn't shown up at least once solely for the paycheck.

The wisdom that Zoe can teach us is that knowing what isn't quite right and continuing the search for a meaningful vocation is one way that battle is won. This isn't some grand statement urging you to quit your job if you're unhappy. Financially, that's not practical for 99 percent of the population. What we can all do is start looking for a better fit while (hopefully) being gainfully employed. That's what I did after spending a year and a half working at a hellish job at a university press. I found an entry-level position at an organization I believed in and worked my way up from there, feeling challenged, trusted, and engaged with the good work being done. Dream jobs are hard to come by. For me, it started as an office assistant position and grew from there.

Zoe's life is balanced in large part because all of her time goes toward work that she believes in, work that she enjoys. Her dream job wasn't handed to her the month she graduated from college. It took years of searching and fine-tuning. Thankfully for her and the countless people she has impacted over the years, Zoe didn't give up.

SOMETHING I WAS VERY INTERESTED in talking to Zoe about was how, after decades as an activist, she managed to avoid burnout—the fate of so many others who spend a few years devoted to a cause and then all but abandon it in exhaustion. Zoe told me, "Becoming a humane educator for me was the actual solution to burnout, depression, despair, apathy—any of those things—because I saw how powerful this work was. I saw the change. It was heartening. It felt great. I felt great. It's a win for me, it's a win for my students, and it's a win for all of the people, animals, and the environment whom they affect." In every possible way, Zoe's particular form of activism nourishes the core of who she is, allowing her to be energized by her work rather than deflated by it.

During her many talks on humane education, Zoe uses the metaphor of a campfire to describe how she stays balanced when constantly learning about so many atrocities. Think of the campfire as Zoe's activism and the topics she teaches about as the fuel. If she spends too much time obsessing over the big problems, there will be too much fuel and her fire will burn the whole forest down. Zoe said about the risk of burning too hot, "If we become the forest fire, what happens? People flee from us. Nobody wants to be near us. We are burning out of control, which is why activists often have such a bad image."

On the other hand, if she doesn't spend enough time thinking about the world and its problems, her drive to make the world a better place will decrease and her fire will go out. When a campfire is tended to just right, everyone wants to sit around it and bask in its warmth. That's the effect she aims to achieve, one that is inviting so that she can inspire others to make positive change. If Zoe lets her anger or sadness over issues overwhelm her, she wouldn't be balanced and she wouldn't be able to inspire others, the very thing that she lives to do.

Activists aren't just known to burn out because of the difficult subjects they immerse themselves in daily. Part of the issue is also that, when it feels like the world is falling apart around you, it's hard to take some much needed personal time to go out and have fun. Some activists work eighty-hour weeks every week, barely claiming any time to care for their own personal happiness. I know many activists like this and watch them as they run around exhausted. They get sick and neglect their relationships with friends and family, all because they are focused on doing everything they can to work toward change. Anyone who has worked within a social movement knows that change usually happens at a glacial pace. Within a few years of activism, we might see small triumphs, but we are unlikely to witness major societal change unless we work within a movement for decades. This can be incredibly frustrating and difficult. As the saying goes, it's a marathon, not a sprint. When going at the pace of a sprint, our energy will undoubtedly fade in the long term. This leads some activists to leave their nonprofit jobs for something less emotionally demanding.

Zoe has been able to spend decades working within a movement that she helped create because she is more than her work. She's a woman who enjoys all the good things that life and this planet have to offer. She told me, "The other thing that's really helped is that I really like having fun. And I do improvisational comedy and I play games, and I do silly things. And I get up and start dancing, you know, regardless of whether anybody else is dancing or not. I do things that are incredibly fun and joy inducing."

During the interview, I learned that Zoe has no shortage of pleasurable activities in her life. She practices aikido up to three times a week, goes hiking at Acadia National Park regularly, spends time with her husband and son, loves ice-skating and snow shoeing, forages for mushrooms, kayaks, and cross-country skis. Her world is more than her activism. It's also worth noting that many of leisure-time activities are physically challenging. They keep her fit and healthy, and they work as stress relief, giving her all the benefits that come with living an active life.

In a world that values productivity and achievements, doing something solely for your own amusement can often feel selfish or frivolous. I've heard friends who have been working themselves into an early grave say in a whisper how they'd love to take thirty minutes to go get a manicure and then in the same breath dismiss the very idea because they have too much to do. How can they go foraging for mushrooms when the rain forest is being chopped down at the very same moment? Having fun and taking a much-needed break shouldn't be seen as selfish. It should be seen as recharging our batteries so we have the ability to keep working on the topics that are so important. Zoe said she feels no guilt when she goes hiking with her husband and dogs. She does her work for her cause during the day and then takes time for herself and her family in the evenings and on weekends. And that's why she's been an activist for more than twenty-five years. Taking care of herself and her own needs hasn't taken anything away from her cause. Instead, it has allowed her to keep going.

IT'S OFTEN SAID THAT KINDNESS is its own reward. And how true that is. The benefits of being kind to others and living in accordance with one's values are so numerous, we might just want to go out and look for a stray dog to rescue or volunteer at a homeless shelter. Zoe is no exception. She figured out long ago that giving through acts of kindness, no matter how simple or small, makes her feel incredible.

When Zoe was a young girl growing up in Manhattan, her parents taught her that how she behaved toward others mattered. She told me, "As a kid growing up in New York City, I was taught by my mother that if there is somebody elderly or disabled, you give them your seat on the bus or the subway. I was just taught that and I always did that and it always felt great. Just something as simple as saying to another human being, 'Would you like my seat?' and then having them sit down and say, 'Thank you so much.' I mean, just so basic, so simple. And I even remember a time when I was in high school, I didn't give my seat to somebody who clearly needed it because I was really tired and I was feeling sort of like a petulant teenager. I felt that lack of generosity and that lack of kindness for a long time. I mean I still remember it to this day. It didn't feel good. And the reverse is just always true."

Many years later Zoe had an experience that reminded her of that very same lesson, and that reminder would influence the course of her life. When Zoe was a sophomore in college, she wasn't making the best decisions. She told me to use my imagination to conjure up all the ways in which she wasn't behaving well. (And then told me to stop imagining, since my imagination was probably worse than reality.) Suffice it to say, she wasn't living up to the person she wanted to be. Around this time she was searching for inner peace. A friend of a friend had traveled to Israel, wound up at the Western Wall, and became an Orthodox Jew. When he came home, he believed that all Jews should be orthodox and went on to try to convince Zoe to alter her beliefs. Zoe, an atheist, was interested in learning and debating theology, so she started taking free courses at New York University during the summer. Zoe was born Jewish but was raised in a secular household. These free classes didn't do anything to alter her belief in God. They did, however, provide a valuable lesson. The rabbi said to her one day at the end of a lengthy debate, "It doesn't matter what you believe. It matters what you do." Zoe described the impact those words had on her. "That comment was pivotal for me. And there I had been doing all these self-destructive things, so focused on me.

This whole idea that it matters what you do, I think, set me on the activist path, on the path of being of service, of doing good in the world. The happy result is that it has brought me a taste of inner peace to greater and lesser degrees that I sought years ago. Not as an end point but as one inevitable outcome of right living."

As Zoe grew older and more informed, she changed more and more of her daily habits to reflect her beliefs. She became a person who tried diligently to live her values. To cause less suffering, she went vegan; she's careful about where she shops so she avoids supporting child labor, slave labor, or sweatshops; she buys used items instead of new; she drinks tap water rather than bottled water; and on and on and on. Each and every day you could probably count fifty or more small and large ways that she has adapted her life to reflect what she calls doing the "most good and the least harm." In other words, Zoe's compassion for humans, animals, and the environment motivated her to make big and small changes in her personal life to best protect all living beings. By living this way, she is able to look at herself in the mirror and know she is someone who tries to live with integrity. She lives the words that the rabbi said to her all those years ago: "It matters what you do."

Living according to her values is also important for the work Zoe does when she's educating others about world issues. She said, "If you're not trying to walk your talk, then it becomes hard to be a role model. It's hard to get anyone to listen to you. If I'm sitting there eating a McDonald's cheeseburger and I'm talking about cruelty to animals, why would anybody listen to me? The truth is that if I ate a cheeseburger every once in a while or if I had bottled water every once in a while, it would make no difference at all in the scheme of things, but if I don't live with integrity, I lose efficacy and I lose self-respect. So for me, integrity just means doing the best to live according to our values."

It's not that she's perfect. In a world as complicated as this one, perfection isn't even an option. Zoe mentioned that even though she knows she should drive as little as possible, she still goes out to Acadia National Park a few times a week to hike. She still buys new things occasionally. When her computer breaks, she'll get a new one. Zoe said, "I drive a Prius, which is better than if I were driving a Hummer, but I'm still driving. I'm still burning fossil fuels so I can take a hike, but hiking is not something I'm willing to give up. Everyone has those things." Zoe knows that it's impossible to live on this planet and not leave any kind of footprint. She simply hopes to make hers as soft as possible.

This lack of perfection, oddly enough, also aids her in her mission to make the world kinder through education because it keeps her humble. She thinks that activists who adopt a holier-than-thou attitude are at risk for becoming arrogant, which impedes them from inspiring others to change their behavior. She told me about her imperfections, "It makes me more forgiving and it makes me more humble. I think that that's important because one of the unbalanced things that happens to activists who completely immerse themselves in whatever issue they are trying to change is, they may have no time or awareness about other issues. They may get very, very, very committed to and self-righteous about their particular issue and lose perspective on all of the ways that they fail because they are so great at being completely humane toward animals or very eco-friendly."

I would say, based on seeing her lifestyle, that Zoe does a remarkable job of living a humane life. Being so well versed in such a vast number of issues means that she's all too aware of how she fails. As we all do. That doesn't stop her from doing her best in a countless variety of ways.

Doing everything she can to live by her philosophy of doing the most good and least harm brings Zoe peace. She knows that for the world to really change for the better, billions of people have to adopt

The research showing how activism contributes to one's own happiness and mental health is almost never ending. In a 2009 article published in *Political Psychology,* researchers Malte Klar and Tim Kasser shared their findings that activism can be positively associated with measures of hedonic, eudaimonic, and social well-being.[14] The beauty of taking part in activism is that you have purpose, a goal, and that you are engaging with a group of like-minded people to achieve that goal. It makes people feel connected to something larger than themselves. Zoe is committed to making the world a better place in all sorts of ways, giving her life direction and importance.

more ethical behaviors. Since she can't control the world, only seek to influence it, it's vital for her well-being that she does everything she can personally to live by her values. She explains, "Integrity brings about its own peace of mind and, for me, that peace of mind is that balance you're talking about. I don't know how I could be a joyful human being without integrity, without trying to every day of my life be a good person. I mean, when do I feel the most ill at ease, the most unbalanced? It's when I'm not living according to my values."

When most people think of city living, they think of buildings, concrete, and honking horns. Zoe did grow up in Manhattan, but even among all the skyscrapers and taxicabs, she was able to find the smallest seed to nurture her love of all things natural. At her nursery school, there was a little patch of soil in the corner of the school yard. That's where Zoe was drawn to as a young child, playing in the dirt, totally transported into the natural world. One day, she happened upon a caterpillar. That little creature sparked so much wonder in her that she brought it home to watch it turn into a butterfly. Although Zoe now knows better than to remove creatures from their natural habitat—if she came upon a caterpillar now, the only thing she might take is a picture—as a curious child, she only wanted to witness what nature had to offer. Zoe told me, "I can't even begin to underestimate the power that nature plays in my life. It feeds my very ability to do my work well."

Zoe no longer lives in the city. Many years ago she moved up to Surrey, Maine, where she cofounded the Institute for Humane Education and surrounded herself with nature. She said that each and every day she feels its benefits and looks around with the same wonder she felt as that little girl who discovered a caterpillar in the middle of New York City. "I garden. I grow a tremendous amount of the food that we eat. We live at the Institute, which is an eight-minute walk to the ocean. On the way I pass a spring-fed pond that is filled all summer long with frogs that make so much noise, it's deafening. I go out there at night with a flashlight and I watch them calling and mating and I take pictures under water of the salamander and frog eggs, and then when they turn into salamanders and frogs."

The restorative power of nature is unparalleled. If it's nice outside and you're inside reading, grab this book and go sit with your back against a tree or on a park bench, smelling the fresh air. It doesn't matter if it's deep in the woods or a city park. Being outside among the birds, grass, and sky is all that's required. Zoe's total immersion into the natural world no doubt brings her peace and helps to provide balance in an often violent world. For her specific job, nature also gives her something else: a reason to fight. She told me, "It is the motivation for all the work that I do. I'm so grateful to have been born onto this incredible planet. The despair I feel in the ways in which we harm others is matched equally by the joy I feel when I'm in the natural world, which is why it's so important that we bring reverence-inducing, awe-inspiring, wonder-enriching experiences to people of all ages, but particularly to young people so that they care enough to want to protect the planet—so that the computer doesn't become the only source of their joy and entertainment and pleasure and fun."

Zoe aims to give children the same love of nature that has fueled her throughout her life. One of my favorite games, especially for young children, is the activity called "Find Your Tree," which Zoe shares with young and old alike. Kids partner up. One of them is blindfolded while the other leads their partner to a tree. The blindfolded child has to feel the tree as high as they can go and all the way down to the bottom, feeling for the texture of the bark, branches, knots, how fat or skinny it is, and so much more to really get to know a tree in a very different way. The children are then led (with many disorienting zigs and zags) back to the starting point where they take off their blindfold and are instructed to go find their tree, using only the information they perceived with their nonvisual senses. It's through these kinds of activities that Zoe has taken her love of nature and used it to inspire countless others to feel the same and to stop and look at nature in a different way.

IN ADDITION TO SHARING HER LIFE with her husband and son, Zoe shares her heart and home with three wonderful rescued dogs and a rescued cat. Anyone who has ever been greeted by tail wags, a big wet nose, a head bump or a purr knows how much a companion animal (or four) can add to one's life. On a cold night, they are always there to snuggle. When we've had a bad day, they lend a sympathetic ear.

They don't care how we look, how smart we are, or how many friends we have. All they want is reciprocal love, a warm bed, and food to eat (preferably the food that's in your hand ready to go into your mouth, not the food in their bowl).

Zoe talked to me about the huge impact her dogs have on her and just how fortunate she is to have found each of them. She said, "I cannot believe how lucky I am to share my life with these amazing creatures who love me so much and whom I love so much. They are the most consistent sources of daily joy in my life."

Bringing a companion animal into your home is one of the best things you can do for your mental well-being and your physical health. One study by psychologists at Miami University and Saint Louis University published in the *Journal of Personality and Social Psychology* discovered remarkable results for those who shared their lives with furry family members. Lead researcher Allen R. McConnell, PhD, said about their findings, "Specifically, pet owners had greater self-esteem, were more physically fit, tended to be less lonely, were more conscientious, were more extraverted, tended to be less fearful and tended to be less preoccupied than non-owners." [15] A previous study by Dr. Judith M. Siegel found that people who have companion animals go to the doctor fewer times per year than those who live without a nonhuman animal friend. [16]

Zoe gains countless benefits from having companion animals in her life. Furthermore, Zoe's animals also fall into another category: helping others. Zoe didn't go to a breeder or a pet store to purchase her dogs. Instead, she rescued them, saving them from a lonely cage at the shelter, a hard life on the street, or potential death.

She told me one story about her dog Elsie and how she ended up as a part of the family. After dismal weather canceled their Memorial Day weekend plans to go camping, Zoe's husband, a veterinarian, went to the office to finish up some work. At the same time he arrived, a volunteer from the local shelter came to pick up a lost dog who had been brought in as a stray. The six-month-old Border Collie mix had been kept at the clinic for ten days with the hope that her family would come find her. They didn't, so she was going to the shelter to be put up for adoption. That's when Zoe's husband called her and asked, "Do you want another dog?" Zoe gave an emphatic no. She explained, "We had three dogs already, two of whom were old, and one of whom had bladder cancer. The last thing we needed was another dog. But I told him he could bring her home for the long weekend, and I'd consider it. On the ride home, he started calling her Little Cupcake. He was already smitten."

You can guess how this story ends. Even though Little Cupcake (which soon became L.C., which turned into Elsie) wasn't housebroken, was a major barker, and needed lots of attention, Zoe and her husband fell in love with her and were more than happy to put the time in to get her on the right path. Now years later, Zoe told me, "I can barely imagine life without her. She is our smartest dog and remains the most intense I've ever had. She bugs her older sister Ruby by trying to herd her, and herds us too. When I awake in the morning, even before I open my eyes or stir, she jumps on the bed, comes in close, and gazes at me. I often open my eyes in the morning to her deep and soulful brown-eyed stare. She gives me hugs, arching her neck ninety degrees behind her as she flings her little black body on me and clasps my arms in hers."

I have always been a person with animals, so I can't imagine what life is like without them. Even right now, my two rescued girls Cthulhu and Magneto are happily snoring at my feet. For years Gary and I tried to convince his mother to adopt a cat. She lived alone and we thought it would be one of the best mutually beneficial relationships she could have. She always dismissed the idea, noting that she didn't want the hassle or the responsibility. She talked about having to spend money to buy food and not wanting to clean out a litter box. That was, until she took in a big gray cat as a favor to a friend. The cat had been dumped on the front steps of a police station and the person who took her in wasn't able to keep her any longer. What started as a temporary babysitting favor soon turned into a friendship she couldn't live without. A few years later, she took in two more feral cats who desperately needed a home. If you saw her living room now, you'd find more seating designed for felines than for humans. She has transformed. Where she used to talk of not wanting to bother with a litter box, she now talks about how Fluffernutter (yes, that's one of the names) sleeps at her feet.

OVER THE YEARS, ZOE HAS IMPLEMENTED many different methods of staying at peace with herself and the greater world. Some come more naturally to her, like living with integrity, hiking, or sharing her home with companion animals. Others have been more deliberate actions that she has worked to develop to help her stay balanced. One such choice was to practice something called passage meditation, written about by Eknath Easwaran. Zoe told me, "I practice passage meditation, which is reciting in your mind great works of either spiritual or moral truth that compel living a life of greater meaning and purpose and goodness."

Zoe memorized about a half an hour's worth of spiritual texts from various traditions and writings by Wendell Berry, e. e. cummings, and even her wise friends, all that reflect the kind of life she wants to lead and the outlook she wants to have. It's essentially filling her mind with positivity and goodness so that she can take it in and keep it, providing relief from some of the darker parts of reality. For the past ten or so years Zoe has called upon this practice when she needed it.

She shared with me one of the pieces she memorized, a prayer from Saint Francis of Assisi:

> Let me be an instrument of peace;
> Where there is hatred, let me sow love;
> Where there is injury, pardon;
> Where there is anger, understanding;
> Where there is fear, courage;
> Where there is doubt, faith;
> Where there is despair, hope;
> Where there is darkness, light;
> Grant that I may not so much seek to be consoled as to console;
> To be understood as to understand;
> To be loved as to love.
> For it is in giving that we receive;
> It is in pardoning that we are pardoned;
> And it is in dying that we are born to eternal life.

Zoe's form of meditation is just one of many. Some swear by transcendental meditation, guided visualization meditation (the type of meditation Cathy practices), vipassana meditation, among the many types out there. Meditation helps calm the body and the mind. Some types focus on language, such as Zoe's form, some on breathing, or on a guided journey.

In one 2011 study, participants were asked to attend an eight-week course on developing mindfulness (described by the study as "awareness of present-moment experiences with a compassionate, non-judgmental stance").[17] The training included sitting meditation and mindful yoga. The researchers found that "participation in MBSR [Mindfulness-Based Stress Reduction] is associated with changes in gray matter concentration in brain regions involved in learning and memory processes, emotion regulation, self-referential processing, and perspective taking." The research on meditation is conclusive. It helps us both physically and mentally and provides benefits like stress reduction. Each type of meditation offers its own benefits. As there are so many different kinds, one can explore and see which works best.

Pastimes designed solely for relaxation or personal growth can often be the most difficult to find time for. Thankfully, meditation can be done from the comfort of one's own home, outside in nature, or really, anywhere. More advanced meditators might find they can do it in a crowded space. It also doesn't have to take up a large amount of time. Zoe memorized about thirty minutes worth of text. For her, that amount of time works. Others might sit and do a different technique for just ten minutes. Unlike other activities that reduce stress and help clear the mind, such as being out in nature and working out, meditation doesn't require a specific wardrobe, shoes, or even leaving one's home. And for an activist who wants to focus on positive ways to influence the world, engaging in some kind of meditation might be a great option.

WHEN I TOLD ACTIVIST FRIENDS that I was writing this chapter, they didn't hide their enthusiasm about getting their hands on it. Many had struggled or were currently struggling to find balance. What struck me most about Zoe was that as much as she cared about the greater world, she also cared about her own life. Her activism didn't hijack all of her time or make her feel guilty about having fun. Because she's able to devote time to her own well-being, I think she's an even better role model than someone who spends every waking moment seeking justice. Zoe exudes confidence and peace and displays a real sense of joy. That's the kind of person others want to emulate. They see a happy woman who is working hard to make the world better and they want to be a part of that. They want to be change-makers because they see that it's vital to the future of the planet and that it can help bring a sense of calm and meaning to their lives.

We all want to be a part of something bigger than ourselves. Activism is a great place to find that meaning. Add to that love, fun, and personal growth—those qualities that feed our hearts and minds—and you've got yourself one heck of a recipe for living an incredible life.

TAKING THE PATH
LESS TRAVELED

◆

*How does someone resist societal
expectations and pressures in order
to live the life of their choosing?*

"You certainly notice the pressure, especially if you don't
really do the usual things: go to high school, and then
go to college, and then get a job, find a girl, get married,
have some kids, get some hobbies, send your kids to
college, and then let them kind of take care of you, see
your grandkids, and then you die. No, that's just never
been the way I've operated."

—*Eric Wicklund*

chapter 5

Eric,

an Unencumbered Explorer

WE ALL KNOW THE RECIPE. College + job + marriage + house + kids = the good life. Unless it doesn't. For countless people around the world, that equation feels more like a prison than a formula for contentment. Wonderful lives come in all shapes and sizes. For some, the traditional life as described above is the ultimate goal, and it really does bring with it the promised feelings of fulfillment and joy. Others have to figure out on their own that the life they've been told to live by parents, friends, movies, and ad agencies just isn't the one for them.

It's a brave move to imagine a different path, especially when society is pushing for conformity. That's why I was so excited to sit down with Eric Wicklund. Eric is a forty-five-year-old single man with no children who has found that his personal satisfaction isn't tied to much of anything outside of himself and his passions, his friends, and his family.

When I parked near his home in Boston, Eric rushed out to make sure that I wouldn't get ticketed or towed due to the confusing signs. After he was sure my car would be safe, we walked over to his apartment in a lovely residential neighborhood in South Boston. Normally, a man in his forties might own his own home and share it with a wife and a couple of kids, but Eric shares his space with roommates who are also his good friends. His entire life fits into his bedroom, the place we settled into for the interview. In it sits a bed, a simple wooden desk, a few plants, plenty of books, Red Sox paraphernalia (he's a die-hard fan), assorted items from his travels, two motorcycle helmets, a kayak paddle, and his computer.

Some might not think they could live in a single room as they grow older, let alone share their common space with friends like they did when they were in their twenties. To me, it looked like the room of a man who has it figured out. He doesn't live this way because he's in financial trouble or because he can't attract a mate. He has a job that he loves, working as an English-as-a-second-language teacher at an international school, and he certainly does date when he finds someone who interests him. He chooses to live this way because it brings him the most joy.

I've met enough people (and have even been one of them) who have followed the well-traveled path long enough to find themselves completely lost—people who settled down because they were the right age or bought a house (guilty) because they were told that's what responsible adults do. I've even met parents who had children because that was the next expected step rather than something they wanted from deep within. Most of us like to think that we make decisions based on what we truly desire, but I see evidence each day to the contrary. Far too many of us are on the path set out for us, not the one we chose. Eric is one of those beautiful rarities who desired an alternate path and actually took it.

Of course, since his independence is one of the key reasons I wanted to interview him, one of my big questions was how societal pressure has impacted him along the way. Eric told me that although there was pressure, he didn't give in to it. He told me, "But you certainly notice the pressure, especially if you don't really do the usual things: go to high school, and then go to college, and then get a job, find a girl, get married, have some kids, get some hobbies, send your kids to college, and then let them kind of take care of you, see your grandkids, and then you die. No, that's just never been the way I've operated."

Eric certainly sees why some people do choose to have families and live more traditional lives. I've seen him in action with his nephew and niece. He is a human jungle gym and perhaps one of the best "fun uncles" I've ever seen. Slender and standing at just over six foot two, he delighted the kids by letting them swing from his arms and by randomly scooping them up off the ground. Being the constant jokester, a label he wears proudly, children naturally adore him. However, loving the children in his family doesn't mean he wants to have his own. Eric said firmly about his child-free stance, "I don't want a kid. What do I want a kid for? I'd need to be convinced why I need a kid. I don't get it. So I've never . . . no, I just never have. I like kids. Kids are fantastic. I can see the value in kids and stuff. I'm not anti-kid; I just don't think it's something for everybody."

Eric isn't alone. More and more people are deciding not to have children. In 2010, a Pew Research report revealed that approximately one in five American women at the end of their childbearing years have not had a child. More and more people are not having children, either by choice or circumstances. That compares to one in ten American women in the 1970s.[18] The movement is called living a "child-free" lifestyle. Not having children allows an adult to have more flexibility and more disposable income to travel, change jobs, spend time pursuing hobbies, and so on. That's not to say the choice is for everyone. Some people dream of being a mother or father and find fulfillment that way. But for those who never dreamed of having children, there are some perks to not conforming to the life others expect.

When it comes to relationships, Eric holds a view that's similar to his child-free stance. He's been in serious relationships, and even lived with someone before, but ultimately it comes down to something he repeated a few times during the interview. He doesn't want to be "tied down." He can be the fun uncle, a good friend, a great brother, and a wonderful son, but all of those functions still give him his autonomy. He said, "I think I'm just very, very independent." Thankfully, he has the right attitude to go with an untraditional life. He told me, "I don't care about what other people think about me; I'm allowed to decide."

He has noticed, though, that it doesn't seem like many people consider those big life decisions to actually be choices. Eric told me that when talking to his students, largely young adults, and the topic of marriage comes up, he sometimes asks, "Do you want to get married?" They respond, "What do you mean, do I *want* to get married? Of course I'm getting married and having kids. You think I'm going to disappoint my mother?" Rather than being viewed as one potential path to consider, it's as if marriage and children are a given in life, something not even to be questioned or that is done to please someone else. If the students had answered that they desired a lifelong partnership, deep enduring love, or a family like the one they had growing up, it would be one thing. Instead, Eric hears that they plan to make these decisions because of demands, whether real or imagined, coming from their parents. I picture them all climbing this huge spiral staircase not realizing that every few steps, there is a door on either side offering a different direction. They are so busy looking up that they don't even give themselves the benefit of a choice. Sure, if they really thought about it, they might still opt for a more traditional life, but some of them might enjoy taking a detour or changing course completely.

Thankfully for Eric, he never had pressure like that coming from his parents. He thinks his sense of freedom about his own life comes from his mother who always gave Eric and his siblings options when they were growing up. It was never, *You have to join the baseball team.* Instead, it was more like, *Would you like to join the baseball team?* He told me, "There was an awful lot of freedom when we were little to kind of make up our minds about how the world was, how it works, and how we wanted to approach it. I've certainly seen some of that in Rolf and Renee [his siblings] as well." He was trusted to think for himself and, in line with that, he wasn't pressured to live the same kind of life as his parents. That freedom to get to know his own mind, his likes and dislikes, helped him to grow up to be a confident adult and to always choose the path he wanted rather than the one that most people followed. It also allowed him to ask the big questions about what he wanted from life and to seriously consider alternative routes.

Beginning in his mid-twenties, Eric has been what I would call a modern-day explorer. After earning his high school diploma, he stayed in New York for five or so years, not doing anything he was particularly passionate about. He had decided at the time not to go to college (again, an example of not following the standard path).

Not finding much he wanted to do in his hometown, he and a friend decided to pack up and drive out west. Not long before the scheduled trip, the friend bailed and so, bravely, Eric went anyway, driving from New York all the way out to San Francisco. After rounding out the Pacific Northwest, he settled in Montana and found work at a bank sorting checks. By now, he was in his mid-twenties and he realized that he wasn't ever going to be able to have the kind of job he really wanted without a college degree. It was then that he decided to go back to school, not because it was expected of him, but because it would help him move his life in the direction he wanted.

Since he had grown to love spending his time hiking in the mountains, seeing bears, and spotting moose, he went to college right in Montana. Before heading west, all of his friends and family had resided in one small town. Living in Montana helped him learn what it was like to make new friends in a place far from home. One could argue that this first expedition outside of his comfort zone gave him the curiosity and drive to keep on exploring.

His next life chapter was even bigger. Eric wanted to learn Spanish, so in 1997 he booked a three-month trip to Chile. He was so in love with the experience of delving into a different culture and learning a new language that after he came back to visit his family and grab some clothes, he turned around and traveled back to Chile to work and live. I asked him, "Did you have a job lined up?" He said, "No, actually I didn't." Eric went on to explain that he went back, knowing a Canadian friend had a spare bedroom that he could live in. He also figured that he would be able to find a job teaching English in Santiago.

And that's exactly what he did. Before traveling to Chile the first time, Eric hardly spoke a word of Spanish. He went down there, as he described it, as "kind of this naive American." He laughed and said, "I actually thought in three months that I could learn Spanish. I had no idea what it took. My first six months down there were tough. I mean, I was always going places, and people didn't know what the hell I was saying or, more commonly, I had no idea what they were saying."

The challenge didn't scare him off. It did the opposite. He explained, "One of the great things about being down there is just the challenge of trying to learn a new language and the culture that goes with it." Learning Spanish wasn't a quick process. It was a solid year before Eric was able to carry on good conversations with other people, a task requiring a whole lot of patience and hard work. He said, "If you're going to live somewhere rather than just visit, it's no fun unless you're learning the local culture and language. Every day is spectacular because you're just like, holy shit, I'm living in this place and speaking a different language. It just opens up a whole new world."

ERIC HAS WHAT I WOULD CALL a boyish wonder about him. It's apparent that he loves learning new things and finds other cultures fascinating. It's why his job teaching English as a second language to international students suits him so well. He has students from Saudi Arabia, Chile, Kazakhstan, Brazil, Mexico, Italy, South Korea, Spain, and countless other countries. What I find incredible is that Eric has found a way to take the things he loves about travel and bring them into his daily life. He said, "It's fascinating to learn how different people are from us; it's just interesting to get to know people who have different value systems."

Since he's unattached, he was first to put his name into the hat to transfer when the school he works for considered expanding with a new location in Hawaii. They ended up deciding against the new branch, but how many people would be able to move a few thousand miles away without consideration of anyone else's needs? How many people would move to a foreign country where they didn't speak the language without even having a job? Could he have done that if he had a child? Probably not. Instead of fearing new things, Eric embraces change. He thrives on moving outside of his comfort zone. That kind of freedom is vital to a person like Eric. He has close ties to friends and family, and acknowledges that those relationships are some of the most important things he has. But, based on past history, if he decided to move again, his friends and loved ones would be excited for him and visit him on his new adventure.

I did ask him if he ever got lonely, recognizing that this question comes from my particular experience as an attached person and might be as ignorant as a parent asking me if I'm lonely because I don't have a child. I told him how comforting it was for me to always have a partner to go to the movies with or to try out a new restaurant. As I write this, Gary is in the next room with his headphones on so as not to disturb me. Every hour or so, we'll transfer one cat to the other person, grab a nibble to share, or simply take a break for a kiss. If one of us has to go to the pharmacy, the other might tag along for the ride. Eric responded, "I still live with some other people, so I do have some very good friends that I do default hang out with if no one else is around." He also vacations with his sister and her family, and has great relationships with his students and coworkers. Eric is in no way a lonely man; in fact, he said he spends so much time with other people that he relishes his alone time.

As a self-proclaimed introvert, he said that spending the entire day teaching can take a lot out of him. After work, to unwind, Eric retreats into nature to scramble up and down rocks and go hiking. He called the great outdoors his "sensory deprivation tank." "Usually when I go hiking, it's right after work. At my job during the day, I really don't have a minute alone—which is fantastic—but it's a nice balance to that I guess. Plus I love to be outside. I can think the most clearly about things out in the woods when I don't see anyone else. And you can do that while you're hiking and climbing on rocks, and that seems perfect to me."

His love of nature started when he was a child growing up in upstate New York. "I kind of grew up out in the country in an area where in the morning your mother would tell you to go outside and come back for dinner if you want. I've just always liked to be out in the woods."

Eric doesn't stop at hiking. Living in a city with easy access to water, he can also be found out on the water in his homemade kayak. Yes, the man made his own boat. He was interested in trying out the sport but wasn't convinced that the five thousand dollars required to purchase a fiberglass kayak was worth it. The place he was living at the time had a massive basement. For roughly one thousand dollars, he utilized his love of math and made his own. Eric explained that he had never worked much with wood, let alone created something other than a square object. Yet that didn't stop him from learning a new skill set. At the end of the experience, Eric had his very own seventeen-foot kayak, a boat he takes out on the water regularly.

It's hearing this kind of initiative that makes me wonder if I could do something like that. It's not as if Eric was an aspiring boat maker. He was curious. He was interested. That led him to spending hours on top of hours working on a single goal. He essentially taught himself a new skill, just like Sungrai taught himself how to fix his Austin-Healey. In some ways, I see similarities between Eric taking on a boat-building project and immersing himself in a different culture to learn a language. He commits to what he is curious about. It's the same for Sungrai and Cathy. They all seem to blossom when facing a challenge or embracing new skills. Unlike others who might feel intimidated and frustrated during the early stages of learning how to do something new, they get excited.

In a 2013 study on the benefits of learning something new, scientists asked 221 adults to take part in a specific activity for fifteen hours per week for three months. Some were asked to try their hand at something new such as digital photography or quilting. Others were told to engage in activities that are more familiar such as doing word puzzles or listening to classical music. At the end of the study, the researchers found that those who had learned a new skill had improved memory function when compared to those who took part in less demanding activities at home. Lead psychological scientist, Denise Park of the University of Texas at Dallas, said about their findings, "It seems it is not enough just to get out and do something—it is important to get out and do something that is unfamiliar and mentally challenging, and that provides broad stimulation mentally and socially. When you are inside your comfort zone you may be outside of the enhancement zone."[19]

Another quality that fascinated me about Eric was his constant reassessment of his behaviors. If something doesn't make sense, he adjusts. He said some readjustments are easy, and some (like his struggle to kick the coffee habit) take longer. The important thing to note is that he's aware if he develops an unhealthy habit and does his best to change his behavior so he constantly improves his lifestyle. It's a way of operating that I don't think many people follow. Instead of fighting against our bad habits, too many of us sheepishly embrace them because they provide comfort.

A perfect example for Eric would be when he got rid of his television. He told me about the appropriately nicknamed idiot box, "Got rid of my TV ten years ago and I haven't had one since. TV just sucks. People sit in front of it, and it's designed to keep you sitting there, force you to watch advertising, and quickly get another program shoved in front of your face. People just melt in front of the TV. Getting rid of the TV, I think, is huge."

It's safe to say that most Americans spend far too much time flipping channels and scrolling through titles on Netflix or other video on demand providers. According to the U.S. Department of Labor, people over fifteen years of age watch on average 2.8 hours a day (or 19.6 hours a week). And I doubt that covers the amount of extra time spent watching cat videos on YouTube. Sometimes, it's a program we're passionate about. Unfortunately, too often TV is used as a mechanism to kill time. Perhaps even worse than that (speaking from experience), I think we're afraid to stop watching it because we're not sure what to do instead. If television were suddenly gone tomorrow, how would you fill your additional twenty or so hours per week?

A 2007 article in the *Journal of Economic Psychology* asks the question, "Does watching TV make us happy?"[20] Authors Bruno Frey, Christine Benesch, and Alois Stutzer point out that unlike other leisure activities, watching TV does not require one to dress, leave the house, or find a friend. And turning it on only requires the push of a button. The authors note, "Watching TV has, compared to other leisure activities, an exceedingly low or nonexistent entry barrier." The authors cite a 2002 study by Robert Kubey and Mihaly Czikszentmihalyi that reveals that 40 percent of adults and 70 percent of teenagers in the United States say they watch too much television. They hypothesize that watching TV is more of a self-control problem than a source of enjoyment, especially considering how much TV people do watch. That's not to say that TV isn't a fun pastime in smaller doses, but perhaps it is less so in the huge quantities that many people watch it.

Oddly enough, as I was writing this section, a friend of mine who loves binge-watching television wrote on social media, "Two weeks, ZERO television. No shows. Period. (This is a big deal, because I love television more than anything else that doesn't breathe and isn't ice cream, and also because this 'love' recently revealed itself to be a de-structive addiction.) The first few days were REALLY hard (I couldn't stop thinking about *The Good Wife*), but after seven days I actually stopped even WANTING to watch. I feel powerful, you guys. I feel like I might be able to do anything."

She told me that the first few days were hard because she had to figure out ways to fill time. She had to come up with alternatives to what, for a long time, had been her day-to-day life. As Eric told me about rethinking the less healthy behaviors in our lives, "You have to really work at it hard. It's easy to get into a habit and not even question it." This, of course, made me think back to Sungrai's ability to create his own satisfaction by taking part in hobbies he loves rather than simply waiting to be entertained. Eric does the same thing. Instead of sitting in front of a television, he might be out hiking or kayaking or spending time with friends.

Eric doesn't only adjust an activity when he finds it is not fulfilling for him. He also keeps a tight rein over how he reacts to negative stimuli. He's a big believer in the notion that "nothing happens good or bad except that your mind makes it that way." What does that mean? He gave a great example in the form of responding to bad drivers, a circumstance everyone, whether pedestrian, cycler, or driver, can probably relate to. "In the city when driving, it's so easy to be yelling 'Move *over!*' Sorry, that's the way we do it in Boston—just being mad at every person who cuts in line." Instead, Eric said he's changed that behavior by instead consciously thinking when someone does something that is rude or frustrating, "Don't even look at that. Look *that* way. Just why would you let something like that bother you? What are you, one car length behind now? Yeah, that was really important. And you're pent up and mad about it?"

Road rage is something that happens with regularity. It's during those mundane moments, when someone cuts you off, or brings twenty-five items into the ten-items-or-less line at the supermarket—silly things that shouldn't get our heart rates elevated—that we can choose how to react. Instead of letting one of life's small frustrations consume us or affect our mood, we can simply (as we'd say on the volleyball court) shake it off. When we accept that these infractions are not all that important, we can choose to put our energy toward other things.

According to Eric, this attitude can apply to just about anything. He even self-corrects when he feels the need to criticize others. Gossiping about the shortcomings of others is all too common. Eric tries to filter out any "gossipy" statements, noting that it's actually bad for him as well as bad for the person who is the target of the gossip. He tells me, "Maybe you could say, 'I'm just blowing off a little steam,' 'I'm not saying it to hurt,' or I don't know, maybe, 'It doesn't matter,' but at some level maybe that negativity just creeps in somewhere." Instead of blindly judging others, he said he tries to imagine what it would be like if he were in their shoes so he can find compassion for them. Caring about a person rather than judging them allows Eric to keep his emotions positive.

What I find so impressive about Eric, and why he is so perfect for this book, is that he truly is choosing the good life. He may have a built-in tendency to gossip or honk the horn, but instead of letting his brain move forward with unchecked negativity, he works to control the temptation to act on it. This way, if he comes across someone unpleasant, that person doesn't ruin his mood. The small moments that have the potential to turn a day sour are ones he shrugs off, not letting that negativity get under his skin.

Eric is more flexible than most people. When some of us make plans (yes, I'm holding up a mirror), we tend to focus on the negative if those plans fall through. Eric isn't that sort of person. He embraces change in all its forms, from big things like moving to a new city or country, to smaller things. During a follow-up conversation, he told me a story that exemplified this way of being. While on a romantic autumn weekend getaway to a resort in southern New Hampshire, Eric and his companion got in his car and drove north to take in the gorgeous views of changing leaves that New England has to offer. As we all know, life doesn't always go as planned. Eric's car broke down about two miles outside of Gorham, a small town in New Hampshire. It was a Saturday afternoon, so no mechanic was available, nor did he know what was wrong with the car or how much the repair would cost. All of their clothes were back at the beautiful resort two hours south. What did Eric and his companion do? They walked into town, booked a much cheaper hotel (the only place available at the time in Gorham), and, wearing the same clothes from Saturday through

Monday, enjoyed the local cuisine and sights. They even took a hike along the Androscoggin River.

Eric said, "I didn't fret for a minute that I was missing work or that the car was broken down." That is what I would call making lemons into lemonade. I can just imagine most people on the side of the road panicking that they are miles from town, that they can't get anyone to fix their car, and that their romantic weekend is ruined. To add another well-worn cliché to this paragraph, Eric embraced the notion that life is what happens when you're busy making plans. Eric expanded, "That would probably be just part of a bigger philosophy of embracing change and seeing change as something positive."

That level of adaptability makes Eric pretty difficult to ruffle. When I first considered Eric for the book, his sister told me a story about him—how she had to cancel his visit at the last minute and how she apologized for the short notice and for having to alter their plans. He said, "That's fine. I'll just go kayaking instead." Eric loved seeing his family when he could. He also loved kayaking so that change of plans didn't ruin anything for him. He would see them a different weekend. No need to get upset or grumble about what would have been.

One could argue that Eric is against clutter of all kinds. Clutter in his mind, in the form of negativity, as well as clutter in his personal space. As I mentioned, he fits his entire life—forty-five years' worth of possessions—into a single room. It's not that Eric is totally unsentimental. If an object is small, he will keep memorabilia in the form of pictures or little souvenirs from his travels, but he limits such collections. Think about what's currently in your basement, your attic, hiding in your junk drawer, still at your parents' house. How many rooms would you need to house all the stuff you own? Eric says about his minimalist existence, "There is something liberating about just getting rid of things. I like to travel light. I don't want to be tied down."

If you met Eric, you'd see that he's a man who prioritizes function over fashion. Because we filmed the interview, his biggest concern was which of his Red Sox hats he should wear since his hair was messy. In other words, he doesn't buy in to the "shop 'til you drop" culture we live in. He doesn't find value in possessions. He prefers experiences.

In a 2003 study, Leaf Van Boven and Thomas Gilovich asked the question: "Do experiences make people happier than material possessions?"[21] The answer was yes. They did two surveys and found that an experiential purchase (think of paying money to take a white water rafting trip, go bowling, or head to the theater) had a more positive impact than buying a material item (like a sweater, computer, or chair). The researchers posited that there were three potential reasons that experiences are preferable to possessions: (1) Experiences are more open to positive reinterpretation; (2) experiences are more central to one's identity; and (3) experiences have greater "social value."

We learn and grow by interacting with others, doing new things, and studying new subjects. For the most part, a possession sits on a desk or on the floor. It can be useful, but it doesn't build memories or improve relationship the way that a night out dancing does. We all need possessions to clothe us and feed us. But when it comes to spending our discretionary money in a way that will improve our lives, we might do better to leave the lovely purse at the store and instead invite a friend to take a cooking class or go to a comedy show.

I mentioned earlier that this battle with stuff is one Gary and I are currently fighting. Do I get rid of those adorable vintage knee-high socks that I have never actually worn? How about the pair of earrings I haven't put on in about ten years? How many winter coats does a person actually need? What about family heirlooms? We've done multiple sweeps through our closets, sold furniture, and donated boxes and boxes of things. We've estimated that around half of our belongings have been kicked to the curb. And yet, we're still purging. Now, all our possessions fit in a 698-square-foot studio apartment; and to us, it's bliss. Once we started thinking that way, that possessions aren't the ticket to living a fulfilling life, the temptation to buy new things became almost nonexistent. For Eric, he won't ask himself, "Do I *want* this?" but instead, "Do I *need* this?" This gives him more time and less stuff to take care of. It also gives him more time and money to do fun activities. Every new iPhone he doesn't purchase gives him the flexibility of funds to take a weekend trip with friends.

I THINK WHAT MAKES ERIC SO SUCCESSFUL in achieving a good life, one where he learns and explores new things and has the freedom to do as he pleases, is that he doesn't buy in to the many things that are proven to make us miserable like materialism, overconsumption of television, and inactivity. That, combined with his ability to control how he reacts to negative stimuli, makes him a master at living the life he wants.

When we were finishing up the interview, I asked Eric if he had anything else to add, anything that contributed to his peaceful and balanced state of mind. He told me that beyond anything else, he just wants people to be kind to one another. It's a simple request, and yet, as a species, we have a long way to go. Happily, all of us can start with ourselves and create positivity wherever we go simply by how we choose to interact with the world. Just like Eric.

LIVING FULLY IN THE WORLD AS WE CONTRIBUTE TO IT

•

How do we integrate our work life with our personal life in order to more fully enjoy all the hours in the day?

"When I turned thirty and realized that I wasn't going to live forever, I realized that I didn't want to waste any time. My work life hours *are* life hours. Every day, every minute that I spend in a day, is spent in a way that I want to contribute to the world and I want to experience the world. And I'll tell you that before I turned thirty I was contributing to the world with my time, but I wasn't *experiencing* the world as much with my time. Now I'm focusing on doing both."

—*Leanne Mai-ly Hilgart*

chapter 6

Leanne,

an Ethical Entrepreneur with a Balanced Life

AT GARY'S TWENTIETH HIGH SCHOOL REUNION, I met many of his old classmates, now thirty-eight years old, married with solid careers and a couple of kids. Throughout the evening I cycled through the same questions over and over, "What's your name? Where do you live? What do you do?" It was how people answered the last question that really struck me. "Oh, I'm in insurance; you know, boring." Or, "Yeah, I'm a lawyer. Not really worth talking about." These were people in their late thirties who pursued advanced degrees, had built careers, and were working full-time jobs. Yet they couldn't even muster up the excitement to say one positive thing about their vocations. They appeared thankful to be employed and to have the money to live a comfortable life. I would guess that a few of them had more money than I'll ever see, yet they seemed so bored by their work that talking about it after hours seemed like a chore.

I often get the impression that people in the United States think that liking their job is a bonus rather than the norm, that they think those who find joy in their work are the lucky ones. You may have noticed that the people I interviewed for this book haven't hated their jobs. They haven't even tolerated their jobs. It's just the opposite. Their paid work is part of what keeps them balanced. Their jobs are an extension of who they are as people.

Leanne Mai-ly Hilgart, a thirty-one-year-old entrepreneur from the suburbs of Chicago who currently lives in Brooklyn, is another person who doesn't spend her working life in a miserable stupor for the sake of a paycheck. Like Zoe, Eric, and Cathy, she looked at a variety of professions before figuring out the perfect fit for her. In 2008, Leanne started Vaute Couture, her own ethical fashion label. By ethical, I mean that the clothing is made in the United States by people who are paid a living wage, the materials are environmentally friendly, and no animal products (wool, leather, fur, silk, or down) are used in production. Leanne was determined to make a difference in the world by putting her particular fashion talents to use.

LEANNE DIDN'T GROW UP DREAMING of starting her own fashion label. Her early twenties were spent pursuing a variety of potential careers. The only thing she knew for sure was that whatever career she chose, she wanted it to help animals in some way. She attended DePaul University to obtain her MBA in business, did a marketing internship, and modeled for Ford Models. Leanne said she was lost for a number of years while she tried to figure out how best to use her particular set of skills. In the end, all those random interests she investigated ended up giving her the tools she would need to run her own fashion label. Modeling showed her what went into a fashion show and what was needed for a photo shoot. Her internship in marketing gave her insights on how to best promote her brand. And her education at DePaul gave her the business savvy to develop a business plan that she could sustain when Vaute Couture was born.

When she started her company, she knew that there were plenty of cruelty-free shoes made with leather alternatives, but that wool and down were still the primary products used to make coats. She also knew that birds were plucked while still alive for their feathers and that sheep endured horrible pain and eventual slaughter in the wool industry. By starting a vegan coat business, she could both raise awareness for animals that were largely being overlooked even by the animal rights movement and give people a beautiful and functional coat to wear in the process—a coat that could keep a man or woman warm even in a Chicago winter. She had found her mission: to use fashion as a way to talk about issues that affected animals and to create the most ethical and fashion-forward designs she could.

What started out as a one-woman operation turned into a thriving business that has been written about in *Oprah,* CNN.com, *Veg News,* and countless other publications and news outlets. She now has a flagship store in Brooklyn and a devoted fan base for her coats and clothes all around the world. While all of her business accomplishments are impressive, that kind of success isn't what this book is about. What I really wanted to talk to Leanne about was what it was like for an entrepreneur to build a business from nothing and how she balances her business life with her personal life. It was with that line of questioning that I knew I had struck gold.

Gary and I visited Leanne at her adorable little one-bedroom apartment in Brooklyn. She had just moved in and was living alone for the very first time. Not everything was set up yet, so bits and pieces of her life were scattered along the edge of the floor. Her dog, Audrey, kept alternating between climbing up on my lap and on Gary's as we all settled in on the couch, each with a cup of tea. Even though she said she felt a bit tired, she was all smiles and seemed to be feeding off our positive energy while emitting her own. Leanne said she had reached a point in her life where she was finally feeling in control and balanced, something that was not true just a few years back.

Three years ago from the outside it looked like Leanne was living the dream. She had achieved what so many people crave—a job and mission that she believes in. That very quality I had a hard time finding at Gary's reunion. Leanne said she's always felt passionate about her company and good about what she was putting into the world, but during her early years of running the business, rather than enjoying the process of building something from nothing, she said she was working herself into an early grave. Her mission came first and her own well-being was secondary. Even with a job she loved, she said balance was in short supply.

Leanne described struggling through eighty-hour work weeks, late nights, poor sleep, and not enough hours in the day to do everything she needed to do. She thought that in order to have a successful business, she needed to put 100 percent of her time into the endeavor. The mission, to save animals and raise awareness through her brand, was the only thing that mattered. So she worked nonstop for a few years, and it paid off. She soon had a profitable business, one that was getting great press and that people were excited about. Here she was, successful and proud of her work, and yet, she said she wasn't balanced in the way she knew she could be. Her business was controlling her instead of the other way around. She knew that had to change, did a lot of soul searching, and found the middle ground she was looking for. What she needed was a fundamental shift in how she viewed her working hours and her personal hours.

For years I've heard a particular saying used to describe how people balance their working life and their personal life. It's the question, *Do you work to live or live to work?* Working to live implies that one works in order to fund their real life, the fun part, after hours. The second option, living to work, points to a person who spends their entire life married to their job without having much of a personal life. If I had just these two options, I'd choose working to live, no question. However, there is a third option—one that not enough people talk about, but one that Leanne has discovered is the only way she can live.

You see, Leanne said she doesn't believe in what most people refer to as a work-life balance—the notion that you go to work, do your job, and wait until you punch out before you start your "real" life. She explained, "For me, the work-life balance idea suggests that there are hours that are for work and there are hours that are for life. When you have hours that are for work and you rush through to get to the hours that are your life, you are fast-forwarding through the majority of your life, because the majority of the week as an adult is spent working. When I turned thirty and realized that I wasn't going to live forever, I realized that I didn't want to waste any time. My work life hours *are* life hours. Every day, every minute that I spend in a day, is spent in a way that I want to contribute to the world and I want to experience the world. And I'll tell you that before I turned thirty I was contributing to the world with my time, but I wasn't *experiencing* the world as much with my time. Now I'm focusing on doing both."

Let's break it down. There are 168 hours in a single week. Assuming we sleep a good 8 hours per night and work between 40 and 80 hours per week (yes, many people work 80 hours with one very demanding job or by working multiple jobs). The average American spends about 50 minutes each day commuting to and from work. Using those numbers, we end up with 68 hours of free time at best

A 2013 survey conducted by the company Philips North America found that 96 percent of Americans believe that utilizing their personal interests in their career would make them happier.[22] A whopping 68 percent of Americans would even be willing to take a pay cut to work at such a job. Now, those are beliefs about how people think they would feel. So what about those who are living the reality? The study showed 48 percent of workers who are using their personal interests in the workplace said they were satisfied. The people who aren't able to bring their interests into work? Only 7 percent of them reported being satisfied. The study also suggests that taking a job that incorporates our interests reduces the likelihood that we will regret our career path later. Of the survey respondents, 41 percent without personal interests at work regretted their path, while only 23 percent with personal interests at work regretted their decision.

or at worst 30 to 50 hours of free time in which to eat, play, clean, go to the bathroom, or whatever else we might need or choose to do. For those who don't like their job, that means cramming all their living into that limited pocket of time. That is, unless our work hours count toward our life hours. If we're doing something we love, and not killing ourselves in the process, we have up to 112 "living" hours each week, instead of somewhere between 30 and 68 hours.

Leanne said that when she was in her twenties, the future always looked like it was out in front of her, like there was ample time to figure out how to balance all of her interests. Sure, she was putting in a lot of hours, but they would pay off eventually, right? She'd be able to start enjoying her life more fully at some point. Or so she told herself. At thirty, she came to the startling realization that life wasn't in the future. Life was right at this moment. She asked herself, "When do people become adults? When are those decisions made? They *are* being made. You make them every day. You make those choices every day. How you want to live is not something in the future. Life should never be about the future."

Rather than being a person who sacrificed herself for her company, Leanne changed how she approached her work. Now, instead of separating her life into two sections— work and personal—she decided that every minute should be spent doing things she wanted to do. Her business was a part of her life's work, but it couldn't give her everything she needed. And that meant she had to start running her company in a different way.

That's when she asked herself when in her life she was the happiest. She said the answer was simple; it was when she was a resident advisor in college. If you ever meet Leanne, you'll see right away that she was probably the greatest R.A. you could imagine. She smiles constantly, loves giving hugs, enjoys meeting new people, and, frankly, could best be described as bubbly. She told me, "I loved having a community; I loved bringing out the best in people; I loved being outside and seeing lots of people every day. Those were the things that I loved, but for a few years I thought I didn't have the luxury of even asking myself what do I want in my day because I thought I just have to give everything to my business mission. And once I realized that I wasn't going to last very much longer, I couldn't do that anymore. I then asked myself, 'Okay, well, what are the things that when I do them, I can handle that day?' That's when things changed."

Two years ago, I wouldn't have interviewed Leanne for this book. Sure, she would have had a lot of the different pieces I was looking for in people who were choosing the good life. She had passion for her work, great friends, and a real love of life, but she wasn't taking care of herself in a way that allowed her to enjoy all the wonderful things she had worked for. She was, as she put it, reacting to life rather than being proactive.

Instead of working constantly, Leanne began carving out time for herself. Three very simple things changed the way she felt about her days.

The first was prioritizing sleep. For years, Leanne would stay up late getting work done, go to bed exhausted, and wake up feeling the same. She said the cycle would just repeat ad nauseam, leaving her run down and unable to perform at her best. Now, she makes sure she doesn't do any work at least two hours before bed. That time is reserved for reading, playing with her rescue dog Audrey, watching a movie, enjoying a cup of tea, or doing something else totally unrelated to work. Now eight hours of solid sleep is a must for her so that her body can be ready and healthy for whatever she might encounter the next day. Leanne once read that entrepreneurs need to train like athletes so they can handle the amount of risk that comes with the job.

When athletes have a race the next morning, they are in bed early so they can perform at the top of their game. The same should be true for business owners. Leanne said she now makes sure that no matter what comes her way, her body is prepared. She starts each and every morning feeling refreshed and ready for whatever the day may bring.

The American Psychological Association notes that psychologists and psychiatrists believe not getting enough sleep is one of the most overlooked health problems common among the American public.[23] They also note that getting a solid eight hours regularly can contribute to better memory, a boosted immune system, better concentration skills, and even a decreased risk of being killed in an accident. On the flip side, not getting enough sleep for a prolonged period of time can lead to mood swings, issues with memory and cognitive function, an increase in accidents, and more. No wonder Leanne felt better equipped to run her business with a full night's sleep under her belt.

The second thing that Leanne decided she had to have in her day was interactions with others. As I mentioned, she loves community, which is why she flourished as a college R.A. Working from home by herself wasn't healthy for her. Making small changes so she could be around other people, even if that simply meant bringing her laptop and her work to a coffee shop for a few hours, transformed how she felt. She was no longer isolated. She explained, "I really love sun. I really love people, and I really need to see both of those things every single day, so that's changed a lot of things for me." While Leanne didn't have to be chatting up the other customers, she *did* need to be among other people and sitting next to a window so that she could enjoy the sky.

The third thing she needed to include in her daily life was exercise. She explained, "You have a body. You should probably experience it, and it really is funny how different you feel when you don't exercise. Our bodies are meant to be used." Leanne took up running, a pastime that not only gets her body moving, but also helps with her second requirement, being in the world and seeing sunshine. "I have a really funny voice in my head when I run. And that voice is just like a twelve-year-old who is excited about everything. So I'll be like,

Yay dogs! So anything I see, I'll be like, *Yay sunshine! Yay it's raining!*" If she's not in the mood for running, she looks at the schedule of classes happening at her gym during a window of free time and chooses one of them. It could be something she's done before or something totally new. The important part is, she's active and interacting with others.

When people talk about the secret to happiness, as if it's some old piece of wisdom written on a scroll buried beneath the sea, I think about the kinds of things that the people I've interviewed have said. With Leanne, we've got sleep, exercise, and interaction with others. I would say, more than it just being three small things, what she was really missing when her life was out of balance was prioritizing her own needs ahead of her business. Too many people (and I'm going to say it: especially women) associate doing things for themselves with being selfish. As if sleeping in late or getting to the gym is a capital offense. Leanne found that when she gave herself the things she needed, she was in a better position to run her company. She said about the change in her priorities, "I'm not a prisoner to my career, to my mission. Instead it's a symbiotic relationship where the more that I take care of myself, the better I am for my mission."

This isn't just good advice for entrepreneurs; it applies to parents, caretakers, employees, to anyone who puts someone or something else's needs ahead of their own. Of course we want to be giving and help others whenever we can. But it has to come from a place of strength. Always putting oneself second means that balance can never be achieved. Leanne asked herself what she needed to be the person she wants to be. Then, she gave herself those things. That's a question we should all ask ourselves on a regular basis. What do I need that I'm not currently getting? Time with friends, healthy food, enough sleep, time alone (shout out to all the parents out there), time to read, to cook, to play? Once we identify those things that we're not currently getting but we know could make us happier, that's when we have to break old habits and say yes to ourselves and our own needs— even if it means having to say no to others sometimes.

I WAS VERY CURIOUS HOW THE LIFE of an entrepreneur would differ from that of an employee. There is a lot more responsibility that comes with running one's own business, and with responsibility can often come stress and anxiety. Leanne started Vaute Couture completely self-funded, and she worked long hours for years to turn it into the thriving business it is today. She now has employees to help her, but no matter what happens, good or bad, the responsibility rests on her shoulders. Not everyone is built for that kind of pressure.

I asked Leanne the question I had asked so many others throughout the interviews—the issue that many of us struggle with and are learning to manage: worrying. Sungrai and Emery had their own way of handling worry. They always do things to the best of their abilities and don't obsess over things that are out of their control. Leanne's method is quite similar. With a whole company to take care of and a lot more risk and uncertainty in her daily life than many of us face, hers has a bit of a twist. She told me, "I used to worry when something would come up that seemed worrisome, and then I realized that everything was always okay. I should instead just know in my brain that, with the life that I lead and the risks that I take, there is always going to be 30 percent that I could worry about. But since everything is already okay anyway, I don't need to worry about it because it will be fine. So there is that 30 percent that I just know is there and I'm okay with it because I literally won't think about it."

In a study examining optimism and pessimism among women, researchers found that optimistic outlooks reduced one's risk for heart disease and of dying in general.[24] Those who displayed cynical hostility, meaning they held hostile thoughts toward others and had a broad mistrust of other people, were at an increased risk of dying. Other studies have shown that dispositional optimism decreases feelings of loneliness over time and is associated with less severe reactions to pain.[25]

What does she mean that everything will always be okay? Not all of the problems she encounters wind up with positive outcomes. Leanne, an optimist by nature, knows that one thing going wrong will very likely not be the end of her world or her company. She'll get through it, figure it out, fix what she can, and move on to the next challenge. Worrying solves nothing. She said, "When I let myself worry about it, it was worse or just as bad as if something bad had happened. So once I realized that, I don't waste any of my time worrying about things. As long as I know I'm living my life with integrity, then there is nothing to worry about. As long as I know that I'm doing everything right as best I can, then I don't have to worry about anything."

It also helps that Leanne is a self-described solutions person. When presented with a challenge, she looks at it as an opportunity rather than an obstacle. As she sipped her tea with Audrey on her lap, Leanne told me the sweetest example of turning lemons into lemonade I have ever heard. Just before Christmas something had gone wrong with production. Coats came in but wouldn't be able to be shipped out in time to end up as gifts under the tree on Christmas morning. The holidays are big business for most companies, Vaute Couture included. This hiccup was going to mean having some potentially angry or, at the very least, disappointed customers. That's pretty much a retail nightmare scenario. Leanne said, "If a problem arises, I've got to get in there and figure out the whole situation, and strategize. What am I working with? That is always my question. What are the hidden tools here? What are the opportunities?"

Leanne couldn't fix the entire problem. She knew that. Instead of focusing on what she couldn't do, she came up with an adorable solution to address at least part of the problem. She would load up her car, throw on a Santa hat, and hand-deliver all the coats she could to customers in the New York City area. Many business owners would have emailed out apologies, maybe a coupon, and called it a day. Leanne became Santa Claus, showing up at people's doors to make some surprised customers very happy. She told me, "It's not always easy to go through a challenge, but it's a lot easier when you look at it as an opportunity."

I THINK ONE OF LEANNE'S strongest attributes is her ability to embrace change in all its forms. She knows that every single second everything on this planet is changing—the cells in our bodies, the earth beneath our feet, how we feel. Leanne is a person who gets excited about change, whether it impacts her business or her personal life.

We talked a lot about a seven-year relationship she had in her twenties that ended when she moved to New York City. Leanne got married quite young and thought she'd grow old with her partner and that they would spend all their years on earth as a twosome. She and her then-husband had committed to the idea of forever. Everyone who saw them believed they were the perfect couple, and they were, for a time, until a major roadblock set them on different paths. Leanne said, "We started getting to the point where we were thinking about having kids in the future." For many, the idea of starting a family is exciting. For these two, it was full of strife. Leanne's partner came from a very religious family. Leanne is spiritual, but doesn't subscribe to one particular faith. The fact that her husband's family was religious wasn't the problem. The problem was that they wanted to convert her. She told me, "I realized that when we would leave his parents' house, we would be very stressed out and that it made him feel like an outsider in his own family. And that was very hard for me because I didn't want to be a part of that pain for him, and at the same time it was creating pain for us, between us. And then I thought, *What if I bring a child into this situation?* Now we could break up and have had these wonderful seven years together and we'd be okay. But let's say we have a child and then we realize that it's not working and it's a situation where his family really wants me converted and their grandchild converted. I would not want to take that risk. And so once I realized that, there wasn't really any other choice. Once it's someone else's life, I can't make that decision for that future child."

They gave themselves six months together to do all the things they wanted to do before ending the relationship—after all, love wasn't the problem—and then Leanne followed her dream and moved to Brooklyn. The process was painful, but also exciting. She simultaneously mourned the loss of her relationship and felt eager to start a new chapter in her life. She said, "While we had had a wonderful time together and had been so important to each other and I would not be the person I am without him, we were not meant to hold on into the next stage of life. If we had, we certainly would not be breaking up under such good terms because by that point, we would probably resent each other and have a very muddy scenario having a child involved."

For Leanne, the risk of the unknown isn't a good enough reason to stay stationary. She explained, "You hold on to how things used to be instead of moving forward. Things always change. So either they're changing in a positive way and you're still in alignment, or they're changing in another way and you're not in alignment and you're holding on to something that's holding you back and keeping you from things that actually are right for you."

I have too many friends who have stayed for years in a relationship, job, or friendship that they knew wasn't right. They would complain. They would wonder what they should do next, and then they would do absolutely nothing. It was like they didn't feel they had a choice. Here they were, chained to something that didn't make them happy, not realizing that the chains didn't actually exist. They could leave whenever they wanted. What were they really afraid of? I would bet my life that it wasn't losing the thing they no longer wanted. Instead, it was fear of change. What if nothing better comes along? What if this is as good as it gets? What if I can't do it all on my own? Leanne gave me her theory: "I've noticed that people in general have a very strong attachment to what they have, no matter what it is. Why do we do that? Why do we look at something and say, 'I want this; I'm going to try so, so, so hard,' when, if it's not working, it's not working? Stop. Just stop, you know. Stop trying so hard. You don't need to try so hard. When something is right, it will work."

Leanne said she believes that just because something was a good fit for someone in the past, that doesn't mean it will be right forever. She explained, "Life is about choice and that's something I'm realizing a lot this year. If you don't have freedom to choose what you're in, what you're doing, who you're with, then that experience will be a lot less enjoyable, a lot less fun, for you or for both of you if it's a relationship. Once I know that something is not right—it doesn't feel expansive anymore; it doesn't feel energizing anymore—I just move on."

This was a lesson Leanne learned early on. She had always been good at moving forward if something wasn't working, but in her younger years, she did almost continue on a path to make others happy, something she wouldn't dream of doing now. Before Vaute Couture and business school, Leanne tried her hand at teaching. She told me, "I thought I wanted to go into education because it made the most sense in terms of spreading awareness and making the most of people, helping them bring out the best in them." Education turned out to be a bad fit; Leanne was miserable. Still, she felt pressured to continue down a path she knew was wrong for her. That's when her partner (yes, that same one from the seven-year relationship) said, "Listen, you don't have to do this." Leanne recalled, "And I thought, *Well my parents helped me pay for school. I have to at least give it a year*, and he was like, 'You're over it.'"

If Leanne had stayed in education, she would have been settling. She would have done it just so she wouldn't have felt guilty about wasting her parents' money. Her spouse helped give her the strength to do what she knew was right—to move on and find the career that would make her happiest. We have one life. Why would we spend one more minute than we have to pursuing a profession or a relationship that we don't want? I think Leanne hit it on the nose. It's because, to use a well-worn cliché, most of us choose the devil we know over the devil we don't. We may end up miserable, but we're paralyzed to do something about it.

If you feel like this speaks to you, to your life, ask yourself the same question Leanne asks herself. *Does this (insert job, person, hobby) energize me or drain me?* If it energizes you, keep doing it. Relish it. If it drains you, perhaps it's time to reconsider whether it's still something you should have in your life. Change can be scary. I'm a person who fears change. I'll admit it. I've learned that the fear I feel can't impact my decision making. Instead of listening to the voice that tells me I should stay put, play it safe, I ask myself what I really want. And then I do what I can to make that other path, the one my heart desires, into a reality. Taking risks is scary. Living a life holding on to jobs and people who no longer make you happy? That can be a whole lot scarier.

ALTHOUGH LEANNE USES MEDITATION now to keep her life in balance, she said she didn't always understand its benefits. Growing up, her parents even had an entire room devoted to the practice, and still, Leanne just sort of shrugged it off until they convinced her to go to a retreat led by peace activist, teacher, and admired Zen Buddhist Thich Nhat Hanh. Now, knowing Leanne, I can say that even if meditation hadn't been a part of the retreat, she would have still been totally mesmerized by a man with that kind of background. Peace activist? Human rights champion? That's right in her wheelhouse.

At the retreat, Leanne learned how important it is to stay in the present. Thich Nhat Hanh had a very specific tool for this, something called the Bell of Mindfulness. At various points throughout the day, a bell would ring and everyone who heard it stopped, listened, felt his or her breathing, and embraced a sense of calm. This was especially powerful for Leanne. She said the bell would ring every couple of hours. "If you were working or if you were eating or if you were talking, everybody stopped for like three breaths and literally nine hundred people would stop, stop chewing, stop everything, and the things you would see when you stopped were magical." She described one time when she stopped and "could see the leaves falling from these massive trees in slow motion while everybody stood still." She said it made her think differently about how she experienced time.

Even after the retreat, Leanne has kept this practice in her life, now with her dog Audrey in many ways acting like her bell, reminding her to be in the present and to stop to see what's right in front of her. She said, "It's funny because there is so much beauty in this world and we don't even look at it. We don't even notice it. We act entitled like it's not enough, or we're too much in a rush to see it when that's what we're here for, is to see it. So the bell brings you to the present to remind you you're in this body, you're lucky to be here, this is all for you, enjoy all of it. And Audrey and animals, they're so brilliant at being present. What's more important than everything happening right now? That's one thing really special that animals can give us. Audrey does that for me."

The beautiful thing about the bell as a form of bringing ourselves back to the present is that it doesn't have to be a big bell at a monastery. It could be something as simple as hearing a phone ring, an airplane going overhead, church bells, or setting an alarm on our watch or phone to go off at different points throughout the day. Incorporating small reminders to get out of our heads and focus on our breathing, our surroundings, can, according to Nhat Hanh, help us restore our own sense of peace and calm.

While living in the moment 100 percent of the time is impossible, it turns out that we feel happier during those moments when we are focused on what's right in front of us.[26] Doctoral candidate Matthew Killingsworth and Harvard psychologist Daniel Gilbert launched the website TrackYourHappiness.org to find out what truly makes people happy. Subjects signed up and reported how they were feeling throughout the day, and whether or not they were daydreaming or focused on the activity before them. According to their research, participants were unhappier when their minds wandered, whether that wandering was about planning dinner for that night or daydreaming about a future or past experience. They found that those who were living in the moment reported being happier than those who didn't live in the moment.[27]

Since my interview with Leanne, I've tried the meditative technique she described. I'm a person who is prone to living inside my head. I always have a running dialogue going on about one thing or another. Still, I remind myself to just stop for a second—stop working, stop thinking, stop planning—and just feel my body and my breathing wherever I am. If I'm outside, I look up to the sky and see the cloud formations. Forcing myself to be present without any thoughts other than what is happening right now reduces my stress levels. It makes me less anxious, because in the moment, nothing is wrong. I'm just happy to exist. Leanne said about this phenomenon, "I got it, and it was something where I realized that they always talk about breathing and the reason why is that breathing is a way to remind yourself that you have a body and that you're very lucky to have a body and very lucky to live in this world. And then when you think about that, you realize that all the little things that you're worried about are impermanent and really unimportant. What's real is here; what's real is the physical and connecting experience you have with the world you're in right now."

If you remember what Leanne thinks when she's running—*Yay dogs! Yay sunshine!*—you'll note that she lives in the moment, enjoying the world around her instead of living inside her head. As she runs, her brain is clear. Without the worries of the world spinning around and cluttering her mind, Leanne is able to experience flow in her life. Just like Sungrai. She knows that the present is the only time one can achieve anything.

LEANNE ONLY KNOWS HOW to do things one way: with integrity. She has that in common with everyone else featured in this book. In some ways, it might be the most important connection they all share. I think this integrity, or kindness, or honesty comes down to wanting to live in line with one's ethics, because to do otherwise would to be out of balance, like saying or believing one thing and doing another. Zoe talked a lot about the need to stay true to her values. Not because of outside forces, but because she felt her best when she was acting ethically. Leanne was no different. She told me, "When I was a kid, I realized that I was a really bad liar. The second that I know that it's some sort of deception or something that could actually harm someone or something that's selfish, it makes me very uncomfortable."

Do you know that feeling? That squeamish awful feeling you have if you're doing something unethical, or that you know isn't your best? It could be as small as throwing out a plastic bottle because recycling it would require an extra step, or telling a lie because the truth would make you look bad. Each of the people I talked to did their very best to do no harm. They were highly moral people, without being preachy, without judging others. And that is something we can all strive to do. It's not about perfection. Leanne said, "Obviously I'm not perfect. I make a million mistakes and I know that, but if I know that I'm doing what I can, I can then find out what the better situation is and then make it right. I don't even know what the alternative is. It would just be really heavy and uncomfortable. Why would anyone want to do that?"

Unless we're sociopaths, living out of alignment with our values is going to feel awful. And yet, so many of us do it. People cheat on their spouses, cheat on their taxes, cut people off on the highway, tell little white lies and great big ugly ones. People gossip and judge and, at times, speak with the sole intention of hurting another person. I'm with Leanne. Acting without integrity makes me feel like a charlatan. It feels so bad that it's not even worth doing because it will haunt me for days, weeks, or years to come.

Leanne doesn't only practice integrity in her personal life. Her business is also in line with her ethics. She could be making substantially more money by manufacturing her clothing in sweatshops in China and by using cheaper materials instead of making sure her fabrics are eco-friendly. The vast majority of other clothing companies play by those rules. So why didn't Leanne? What she does, paying people a living wage and using eco-friendly materials, is far from the industry standard. But I doubt she'd be able to sleep at night if she knew that children were sewing together her coats. Or if people who had been working all day on her products went home still unable to afford to put food on the table. How about if the dyes used on her clothing polluted the water or if animals suffered and died to become a fabric? She'd be out of balance for her entire life because she'd know that her success was built on selfishness. She said about deciding how to run her business, "I wouldn't have a fashion label if I wasn't able to create with it. Since I don't have a background in fashion, I don't know how things are normally done really, so instead I start from scratch and say how do I want things done? How do I want workers to be treated? How can I choose fabrics that are good for the environment, and if I can't, then how do I find them or how do I develop them? There's really no other way for me to do it."

Ideally, anything we do in life should align with our ethics. I was in the car a few years ago with Gary and two of our friends and we were talking about investing our money. I mentioned that I put all my money into socially responsible mutual funds so that my hard-earned cash wasn't going to support things like tobacco or defense. One of our friends very bluntly expressed his opinion that by not investing my money in the highest yielding mutual fund, I was hurting my family. I thought, *How could investing in a mutual fund that held itself to a higher standard be bad for my family? What's my ultimate goal? Making as much money as I can at someone else's expense? Or is my goal to prepare for my future in a way that I could feel good about?*

Often when I'm teaching during my day job with HEART and we're talking about child labor or some other social issue, I'll ask my fifth-graders how they would want to run a business. It's always the same. They want workers to be paid fairly and for the business to treat the environment with care. All of the ideas coming from the mouths of ten-years-olds show a world in which the standard business plan would be to run an ethical business, with people, animals, and the planet as a top priority. Making money is up there too. It just doesn't trump everything else. I often wonder what those same students, some of whom will likely run a company someday, will do when they are older. Will money overpower their ethics? Or will they grow up to be like Leanne and the other people whose stories are in this book? Citizens who care as much about their integrity and the well-being of others as their own bank accounts.

LEANNE WAS BORN INTO THIS WORLD with many of the qualities I was looking for. She's a natural optimist. She loves people. She's compassionate and acts with integrity. Plus, she followed her dream, using the tools she had and her natural abilities to create a job she loves. For years, the big missing piece in her life was figuring out how to take time for herself when she had a business to run, but she mastered that too.

SAYING YES TO LIFE

•

*How do we find our place in the world
while remaining true to ourselves and others?*

"There are few philosophies I live by but honesty is always
up there, and the big part of it is being honest with yourself. I noticed when I was honest with myself and about
myself to others, that's when good things come."

—*Michal Trzaska*

chapter 7

Michal,

*an Honest Man Living Fully and Flexibly
in a Land between Two Countries*

WHEN I PULLED UP TO MICHAL (pronounced "Me-how") Trzaska's
house, I was entering a familiar space. Unlike all of the other interview subjects I had met with until that point, Michal was someone
I knew and considered to be a friend. I didn't know him well, but
we've gone to movies together, worked on a short film, and shared
a whole lot of meals. He even volunteered to use his skills as a film
editor and designer to help the organization I work for cut together
two educational videos. I always enjoyed his company and saw from
how he interacted with people and reacted to stressful situations that
this was a man who knew how to keep it together. Even when facing
a problem, Michal was always kind, patient, and thoughtful. Never
once did I see him get ruffled.

Our previous get-togethers were always in a group setting. We had
never really sat down, just the two of us, to talk and learn more about
each other. So I was nervous when I entered his home in Hartsdale,
New York. It's one thing to ask a stranger personal questions. It's
quite another to ask someone you know intimate questions about
their perspectives on life, the mistakes they have made, and what
they have learned from those mistakes. It turned out I had nothing
to worry about. If anything, the interview made me even more impressed and more thankful that I already counted this man among
the people I know and care about.

Once we finished eating our takeout food from a local Indian restaurant, we settled into the living room. Michal rents a room in a house close to where he works as an editor for the United States Tennis Association, and his roommate/landlord wasn't due back until 10:00 p.m. We had the place to ourselves. Unlike previous interviews, I didn't have an angle for Michal's story from the start. No particular earth-shattering hardship or struggle. I only knew that he had achieved what I was looking for, something hard to describe but easy to recognize. And at just thirty years old, this man had done it in a remarkably short amount of time. Michal is a person at peace with the world and at peace with himself. Wonder what major quality allowed him to attain this sense of balance at such an early age? In a word: flexibility.

From a very early age, Michal had to learn to adapt to large changes in his life. Born in Poland in 1983, Michal immigrated to the United States with his family to start, as he put it, "a better life for me and my sister." Even though they had a greater chance of winning the lottery than getting a nationalization visa from the United States, his mother applied anyway. Three months later, they were invited in for an interview and offered the chance to move. His parents asked Michal and his sister if they wanted to leave Poland; if they didn't, his parents said that one of them would leave to earn extra money in the United States and then come back to switch with the other parent. Michal and his sister chose not to separate their family, and so, at the age of ten, the Trzaskas relocated from Lomza, Poland, to New Britain, Connecticut.

Imagine a ten-year-old child fluent only in Polish moving to a new country where he couldn't speak the language and was unfamiliar with the customs. And yet, Michal said he wasn't scared. He was excited. Sure there were difficulties and perhaps a bit of culture shock. Just like his adult self, Michal was up to the challenge as a child, embracing the task of learning English and becoming a part of his new home, his first major life lesson in embracing change. It helped that his parents chose to soften the disruption in their lives by moving to a place Michal jokingly referred to as "New Britski" (New Britain, Connecticut). Michal added the common Polish suffix "ski" to the town name to signify the large Polish population in the area, something that would ultimately help him settle in. Upon their arrival, Michal made two Polish friends who helped him learn the ways of a new country. However, he was old enough to remember his life back in Poland.

As a girl with a foreign mother, I have often heard my mom say that she sometimes feels like she doesn't have a home. She was born and raised in England, traveled in her late teens and early twenties, and then came to the United States to live permanently when she was thirty-two. In the States she is often asked, "Where are you from?" since she has an accent. Yet her accent is noticeably diluted, and so when she travels back to England, she isn't really seen as being English. I asked Michal if he related to my mother's experience. (He still has the slightest of accents.) He laughed and said about the sensation, "I call it no-man's-land."

Michal explained that he feels neither fully Polish nor fully American. He resides someplace in between. Coming to the United States as a boy, he took steps to make sure he held on to Poland. He told me, "I refused to go by Michael or Mike so I could hold on to my Polish cultural identity." He continued, "Even though I've been in the United States longer, I still feel very much so like a Pole because when I go home, we still speak, eat, and breathe the culture."

By keeping parts of his Polish heritage intact, Michal has found a comfortable place living in the land between two countries. He is both a Pole and an American but knows that he can't full identify with either group. He said, "There are still aspects of being American that I have a hard time relating to and aspects of the life that my cousins have in Poland that I can't relate to anymore. That's not me."

Some would try and fit themselves only into the current world they are in. That's one of the things that's so special about Michal. He doesn't compromise who he is to make other people comfortable. Not that he wishes to make anyone uncomfortable. However, I've seen many school-age children abandon their given name, not because they wanted to, but because it was difficult for a teacher to pronounce. Not Michal. He even wrote an essay for his speech assignment his senior year titled "My name is Michal, not Michael, Mike or Mikey" to drive the point home. It took time, especially as he was making the transition, learning English and getting used to a new country. Twenty years later he is living comfortably in the middle with a merged identity.

Not compromising himself for the sake of others is a quality we talked a lot about. It stems from one of the values that's most important to him. He said, "There are few philosophies I live by but honesty is always up there and the big part of it is being honest with yourself. I noticed when I was honest with myself and about myself to others, that's when good things come." He gave me the example of being interviewed for a job at a production house and being asked the question that most job hunters dread: *What's your biggest weakness?* Michal explained, "It's the question that everyone hates because you're supposed to turn it into a strength. I simply said, 'I can't spell, and it's a problem because I create on-screen graphics and things get spelled wrong sometimes . . . so we're going to have to deal with that if I'm hired.'" For some companies, that could have been a deal breaker. For this production house, it's what landed him the job. He said, "Later on I found out that was the reason I was hired, because I didn't give a BS answer. I was just honest about it. And it's certainly not easy to say those kind of things to someone you just met."

Michal hasn't always let honesty lead him. As he told me, "I lied before plenty of times as a kid and as an adult, and I found out that it made my life more difficult." The big life event that changed his behavior and made honesty one of the most important forces in his life happened a few years ago. He said, "When I cheated on my girlfriend and then I came clean, it felt good to come clean. It was a big lie, and after that experience, I just didn't want to be in that situation ever again."

He didn't tell his girlfriend right away. In fact, there was quite a bit of time between the act and the confession. Michal had justified it in his mind. After he cheated, he told himself it would never happen again and tried to move on. Once he did tell her (after a mixture of confrontation, guilt, and wanting to be fully open), he assumed the relationship would be over. He explained, "She handled it better than I did because my initial reaction was, 'Okay, it's over. I'm sorry.' But she was like 'Whoa, whoa, whoa, no. First of all, you're not off the hook that easy. Second . . . I want to find out what happened and make the decision if it is over or not.'"

It was around that time that Michal had chosen to make honesty a guiding force in his life. The experience also showed him that even when problems seem insurmountable, telling the truth is a way to help him through challenging and emotional circumstances. He said, "It also taught me that difficult situations can be handled in many different ways. And just because you make a mistake doesn't mean that people will run away from you or you should run away from them, and just because someone else makes a mistake you shouldn't run away from them either."

The relationship has since ended, but not because of anything related to the cheating. The lessons he took away from that entire experience have influenced his new relationships. Michal tries to be clear about how he's feeling so that he's not compromising himself or someone else's needs. He told me, "Honesty helps to keep the drama away. Honesty makes for a better relationship because you're able to be yourself." If he's open and the other person doesn't like what they hear, at least he knows that this isn't the relationship for him.

So many people try to present a version of themselves that isn't exactly truthful during the early part of a courtship, and then they get frustrated when the relationship doesn't work out. Perhaps that's why people always say it's better to be friends first. Friends tend to show each other their more vulnerable and imperfect selves, whereas new lovers can sometimes show the censored version. If a friend loves and accepts us and then a relationship turns to romantic love, we know that it's going forward warts and all. Not a single one of us comes baggage free.

Michal tries to bypass that whole mess by not hiding something in a relationship when it's new. He strives to be open and to assess with a clear head if the person he's seeing is right for him, and vice versa. Honesty is the only way to achieve what he's trying to do. Lying or hiding would just delay the inevitable—a messy breakup with hurt feelings.

I remember being on a first date in my early twenties. The topic of drugs came up so I asked casually, "Do you do drugs?" My date replied, "I don't think I'm going to answer that." For me, drug use, even if it was mild, would be a deal breaker. Perhaps he sensed that, which is why he didn't want to answer. My question then became,

Researchers from the University of Notre Dame found that telling the truth had substantial physical and mental health benefits.[28] They looked at 110 people ranging in age from eighteen to seventy-one over a ten-week period. The researchers started simply by finding out, using a polygraph machine, how many lies, both big and small, participants told during an average week. Anita Kelly, the lead author noted that most Americans lie an average of eleven times per week. In this study, half of the subjects were asked to stop lying. Those who reduced their lies to fewer than three per week showed a reduction in mental health issues as well as fewer physical complaints. The researchers also found that personal relationships improved and social interactions went more smoothly when people lied less.

Is there any point of hiding something big, especially on a first date? Why keep moving forward if from the get-go there is something that would ruin any potential relationship? I think Michal would agree. Honesty and open communication do indeed keep the drama away. It allows everyone involved to be themselves without the fear of being found out. Honesty removes the anxiety one feels when he or she is keeping a secret, and if there is a problem, it allows that problem to be addressed from the start.

Not that Michal blurts out his innermost secrets on a first date. He uses his judgment and as issues come up, he discusses them. As with all things, there is a time and a place.

MICHAL HAS ALWAYS BEEN, as he would describe it, a pretty laid-back person. It's that flexibility I spoke about early on and it's the major quality that drew me to him. He strives to maintain his center, using his incredible skills in emotional intelligence to help regulate his moods. He laughed and said, "It frustrates my mom. She says, 'You're always like, *whatever* and you're indifferent about things and you're happy. If I make this meal, you'll like it. If I make that meal, you'll like it. If we go here, great; if we don't, no big deal either.'" He said he wouldn't describe this as indifference; to him it's about contentment.

When I took a class on Buddhism in college, I learned about something called *almsfood*. Monks in certain regions would go out with an empty bowl and locals would gain merit by filling those bowls with food. The monks would eat what they were given and feel grateful for the gift of nourishment. They weren't supposed to make requests or state preferences. The monks simply accepted what was given to them with appreciation. I'm not sure if Michal knows about the practice, but I think he'd be perfect at it. Rather than get attached to the idea of what he wants, he is open to accepting what life brings. This characteristic extends to all aspects of his life—not just his mother's cooking.

If someone cancels a ski trip with Michal at the last minute, for example, he'll shrug it off and invite someone else or go alone, much like Eric would. If someone hands him a dish he's never had before, he'll gladly sample it. Even when it comes to things that others might find stressful or aggravating, Michal takes them in stride. Like Eric, he doesn't let the small things rattle him, and like Emery, he doesn't lose his temper.

Growing up, Michal said that his parents would fight a lot. The same went for his aunts and uncles on both sides. Put all of that together, and he witnessed his fair share of adult arguments when he was a child. He explained, "I didn't like the adult world of fighting. It just made people upset, and no one really won arguments." Michal strives to come up with win-win solutions so that everyone's voice is heard. He said, "I don't see why everyone shouldn't get a piece of what they want if not all of it. If one party wins, then you didn't think hard enough."

The basic idea behind win-win solutions is that everyone comes to a compromise so that each person feels like they were heard and that their needs were respected. I often teach children this method as a form of conflict resolution. It helps them try to see a problem from someone else's perspective as well as their own. Because they are trying to be fair and balanced, they often come up with inventive solutions that make everyone happy. Michal's philosophy—that everyone should get at least a piece of what they want—is at the heart of the win-win method. Those who do their best at compromising rather than insisting that they always get their way are better able to keep calm, knowing that shouting isn't going to help. Also, not attaching himself to one particular outcome (much like at his mother's kitchen table), knowing there are likely many viable solutions to any problem, makes him able to resolve conflicts without getting into arguments. He keeps an open mind and doesn't let his emotions get in the way of arriving at a reasonable solution.

MICHAL SAID THAT THE LAST TIME he yelled at someone he was in his teens. His sister had done something to his car she wasn't supposed to, so he did what he had seen so many others do each day. He berated her. The next time he felt the need to yell was when his sister again took his car without asking, not knowing that it wasn't fit for driving and could be dangerous. This time, Michal held his tongue. He told me, "It didn't solve anything so I decided there is no point at yelling at her because it's not going to resolve anything and I wanted to try a new quiet approach. And it worked. I think it's easier to think clearly if you're centered and not yelling and screaming."

As it turns out, Michal is quite an anomaly having figured out how to keep his cool at such an early age. According to a 2005 study titled "Age, Anger Regulation and Well-Being," people become better at managing their anger as they grow older.[29] The findings showed that older adults had fewer post-anger thoughts, had fewer thoughts about revenge, and spent less time reflecting on the cause of their anger. The study also found that older people had an easier time using calming strategies, such as substituting a positive emotion for a negative one or use distraction techniques like counting to ten. This is not to say that younger people aren't able to do the same. Michal is living proof of that. However, it appears that age and experience do help people manage their anger and emotions.

In order to keep his even state of mind, Michal tries to be flexible. If a plan changes or something doesn't go his way, he doesn't get upset. He said very simply, "Flexible things don't get broken." I stopped and looked at him, intrigued by those five simple words and how true they are.

That's one quality I've tried hard to take away from my time with Michal—to be more flexible and accepting when life doesn't go as planned. It used to be that if a friend was fifteen minutes late, I'd get frustrated. I'd sit and stew. *Why are they late? Why haven't they called to give me a heads up?* I'd hold myself to the same standard. If I got caught in traffic on my way to an appointment, I'd get anxious and upset that my plan wasn't going exactly the way I had envisioned it. Michal wouldn't stew. He wouldn't get anxious. Instead, he'd occupy himself with something that he enjoyed while he waited. When the person showed up, he'd be happy to see them. When the traffic subsided, he'd be on his way again.

The truth is, there is very little in this life that we can control, and by trying to make things go exactly the way we want them to, we become rigid and quick to anger. When we adjust our attitude to become more easygoing and recognize that plans change, we are able to adapt and let go of stress. I can't control when someone I have plans with is going to show up. I can control how I feel about them being late. As a chronically early person and as someone who likes to make firm plans, I found making this adjustment to be particularly challenging. During those times when I'm sitting and waiting, choosing to be calm and happy rather than frustrated and irritated has made my world better. My feelings of annoyance do not disturb the person who is late, only myself, so it's in my best interest to stop that negative cycle of thoughts.

REWIRING ONE'S OWN BRAIN ISN'T EASY, but it can be done, and in the long run, using Michal's five simple words will help me in far more situations than the occasional traffic jam. "Flexible things don't get broken." At the heart of it, I think his flexibility is what has enabled him not to lose his temper in more than a decade and to be thrilled with whatever food is in front of him. (He loved my BBQ lentils and smoky miso tofu.) He doesn't marry himself to any particular scenario, and he knows that the only thing he does have control over is how he chooses to feel. I'd rather feel good. Wouldn't you?

When most people think of the words "laid back," they don't usually think of active goal-oriented men and women. They probably think of stoners and layabouts, people who spend their time lying around on their couch with a bag of chips rather than engaging in the world. (Not that we don't all like a good couch and bag of chips every now and then.) Michal has mastered combining his laid-back attitude with his thirst for new experiences. He makes films, sees friends, goes skiing, plays tennis, hits the beach, and travels. What he doesn't do is micromanage an experience, plan everything to the minute, or worry about things not going the way they are supposed to. If something goes wrong, he adapts. His flexibility and attitude allow him to enjoy life more because he's not obsessing about what didn't happen. He's more interested in how to make the most of the moment he's in.

FOR THE MOST PART, being flexible can only bring good things. There is a point where one can be too accommodating. We can run the risk of giving up too many of our own needs for the sake of others. If we're always willing to bend to what other people want, we might find we rarely get what we're hoping for. Michal carefully considers a situation before he decides how to react. Again, this shows his clear-headedness when it comes to conflict. He said, "You have to figure out if it's worth resisting, or if you want to be flexible, or if you just want to move out of the way. I guess, pick your battles. There are times where I've resisted and lost and times I've resisted and won, but resistance takes a lot of energy."

Making those assessments about when he's willing to bend and when he has to take a firmer stance only works because he is intimately familiar with his own mind. If he has a problem, he doesn't suppress it. He doesn't ignore it. He brings it to the surface, looks at it

Ever notice in TV sitcoms that people facing stressful situations tend to make terrible decisions? Just broke up—time to call the ex while intoxicated—you know, typical story lines like that. According to research by Jeremy A. Yip and Stéphane Côté, those characters we love to watch flail around display poor emotional intelligence.[30] The researchers found that people with higher levels of emotional understanding (also known as emotional intelligence) are less likely to allow their current stress to influence their decision making on unrelated topics. For example (and this is my example, not Yip and Côté's), if I were feeling stressed about a marital issue, I wouldn't allow that to impact my decision on whether or not to buy a car. The two are unrelated, so why let my stress about one affect my decision on another? People like Michal, who enjoy an abundance of emotional intelligence, are apt to make better decisions because they are able to look at the problem rationally.

from all angles, and decides how best to proceed. In short, he doesn't run away from his emotions. Even when his emotions are difficult, he embraces them.

Michal said, "My process now is identifying and knowing when I'm sad and then finding the source and then trying to solve it. I think the things that make you happy, like going hiking, being active, doing something creative, hanging out with friends, simply finding the things that make you laugh and stuff like that, those are short-term things that push you in the direction. But I think it's important to identify. I see a problem like sadness, and I want to solve it and find the source of it."

Knowing that we're sad is one thing. Taking steps to change our situation is quite another. How many of us stay in jobs we hate, relationships that don't fulfill us, towns we should have left years ago? Many of us know what the problem is. In a lot of ways identifying it isn't the hard part. It's admitting that we need to do something to address the problem. Sometimes that means taking a risk. Leaving that dead-end relationship/job/friendship. The funny thing about people is that even when we know something is wrong, the solution can feel scarier than the pain. We know the pain. We live with it. What we don't know is what life looks like without it.

Gary and I had hung out with Michal the week before the interview. We learned that he was having relationship troubles with a girl he had been seeing. (Yes, even balanced people have relationship woes.) He was at a crossroads. Do they move forward? Do they slow down? Do they stop? He wasn't sure. As sad as the thought of ending the relationship made him, he was still open to the possibility. He knew that if the problems proved to be too great, no matter how strongly he felt about this girl, he would have to end it. My point is that Michal doesn't hold on because he can't bear to let go. He talked with me and Gary calmly and openly about the positives and the negatives of this relationship and carefully reflected on what was best for both of them.

This brings us full circle. Michal is honest with his emotions. Honest with others and honest with himself. Wanting something, for him, isn't a good enough reason to move forward. He has to make sure that what he's doing is healthy for him.

GARY BEFRIENDED MICHAL not too long after working on a short film together. We started hanging out in groups. Once we got to know him better, the three of us started going to movies and other events together. During that time I noticed that as long as Michal was free, he always said yes to invitations. I loved that about him. He was always up for anything—a hike, the beach, a drag show, some independent movie. It didn't matter. If people were going and he didn't have any conflicting obligations, Michal would be there. I asked him about this wonderful quality, that his first response is always to say yes. "That's because I read a quote that said, 'In life you'll regret the things you didn't do and not the things that you did.' That's so true."

That quote made him reflect on how he used to spend his evenings as a teenager, often in solitude, and how he'd like to spend them as an adult. Michal said, "I started thinking about the time when I was in middle school and a lot of the beginning of high school when I didn't have the language and communication skills and social skills to go out and do things, so I would stay home a lot. Like, Friday night I would be home watching TV and though that was fine in the sense where I didn't regret it, but I also didn't know what I was missing out on. Later in life you find out, yeah man, I could have been out with my friends. I didn't want to be in that situation again. So if I get invited, I try to make it."

This quality is something I've found in every single person I interviewed for this book. When it comes to approaching people about being subjects for a book, there is no better group of people to ask than those who are living the life they want. In short, if they can, they say yes. They are open to new experiences and, as I've discovered, value spending time with others above almost all else. Michal told me, "I was recently told that I like to dance at every party, and I didn't get offended. I got excited. I was like, yeah I do. Hell yeah. If I could, I *would* dance at every party."

It's Michal's zest for life, and for experiencing new things that I find so wonderfully appealing. He could be hanging out one-on-one or at a huge concert and be just as happy either way. Just as long as he's out there doing things. He values his time with friends and family as well as looking to form new relationships. When he first moved to New York after living in Connecticut for most of his life, Michal joined a hiking group to explore the area and meet new people with similar interests (okay, and to meet girls). He also started playing tennis with his coworkers at the United States Tennis Association. When Gary was doing the New York City forty-eight-hour film festival, Michal was the first person to sign on to spending his weekend with a group of strangers to create something new. All of this to say, yes, he does indeed dance at every party.

IF WE ARE TRULY TO SAY YES to almost anything, we need to be willing to step outside our comfort zone to try something new. For some, that's a scary thought. For Michal, it's exactly the kind of place he likes to be. "Anything that I know will scare me to an extreme I kind of want to seek out, because it kind of gets you ready to stay cool for everyday life. If I did this, come on, you have to be able to handle this little problem. That's why I seek out those situations."

When I was a child, I was afraid of anything new. My parents signed me up for basketball, T-ball, summer camps, and various other activities that would broaden my horizons. I always rebelled at first, then ended up going. Ninety percent of the time, within two hours of the event or activity starting, I would be thankful I was there. It's never easy to try something new. What if we're bad at it? What if no one likes us? What if we mortify ourselves by doing something wrong? I'd like to say that those childhood fears change as we get older, but many of us are still afraid to try something new. I still get scared. Now, I know enough to do it anyway and not let my fear stop me. Just like when I was a child, I'm usually happy that I ignored my fear.

A lot of that panic and anxiety comes from wanting to impress others, even at things we've never done before. Michal helped me to reassess that desire by explaining that he relishes not being the best. If he's the smartest, most skilled person in the room, he says, "There is no one else to help you grow." He'd much prefer to be one of the least experienced in the room, so that he can learn from all of the other more accomplished people. It's not vanity that drives Michal. He's not striving to impress. He wants to learn. Removing that desire to be seen as an expert about absolutely everything enables him to focus on learning and bettering himself rather than showing off.

Once our ego is no longer a concern, we can open ourselves up to whole new worlds.

Michal still has a list of things he wants to learn. Among them, he'd like to speak French, create an animated film, rebuild a car, and construct his own weekend cabin from scratch. I told him about Sungrai's tactic, to learn something new every year, and that he had rebuilt an Austin-Healey. Michal responded, "That's awesome." I'm sure Eric and Zoe would also join in their "learn new things" party. I could picture them all working on a project together, each of them bringing their own curiosity and excitement to the task, as well as their patience, as they immerse themselves in a new world.

THESE NEXT TWO PIECES from Michal's life are going to feel like old news by now, so I won't delve too deeply. Let's just say that nature and maintaining an active lifestyle are far and away two of the biggest re- curring themes in the lives of the people I interviewed. Most of them like to combine the two and take advantage of outdoor activities like hiking and running. Michal is no exception.

During his first decade of life in Poland, he often went foraging for mushrooms with his grandfather. If it rained, they would be out the next morning searching for new growth. Michal kept those early experiences with him when he attended school to study design. He told me, "Nature has always been a comfort zone for me and also a source of inspiration. Whenever we had a project in art school, to think of something creative I would always go to the beach or go to the woods."

Just like all of the others in this book, being active and keeping fit is also a big part of Michal's life. He enjoys running, hiking, and play- ing tennis. This year he fought against the cold and continued run- ning outside even when the temperature dropped. As I mentioned earlier, he used his love for staying active outside to meet others by joining a hiking meet-up group near his home.

MICHAL ENJOYS HIS JOB, his friends, and his family. He pursues his in- terests, loves to learn, and leads an active life, all of which are worthy of review all by themselves. He was by far the most laid-back person I interviewed. In fact, he's possibly the most laid-back person I've ever met in my life. What he has to teach, what gives him the good life he's made for himself, is all internal and revolves around his ability to adapt to almost any circumstance. At a party, he'd be the guy who could talk to anyone. Michal's flexibility and open attitude toward the world can largely be attributed to his emotional intelligence. He isn't prone to reacting to problems with frustration. Instead, he evaluates and deals with the issues he encounters without a cloud of anger impairing his judgment. I believe it's this levelheadedness that brings Michal so much peace and joy, a quality I think we can all aspire to.

MOVING FORWARD
AFTER THE LOSS
OF A LOVED ONE

·

How do we put the pieces of our life
back together after someone we love dies?

"It's not like how it was. It's really weird. It's like really,
someone took your life and broke it and then you've got
to put things together. And it's not the way it was at all.
That's what I'm learning now. I feel it's easier going when
I realize, *Okay, these are fragments of something very new,*
not compare it so much to how it was with Holger and
Olivia. . . . We love them. We love them like crazy
and that doesn't change and we're going to keep thinking
about them every day and love them, but this is what
we have in our little family right now. Let's see how we
move on."

—*Daphne Yeager-Ostendorf*

chapter 8

Daphne,

a Filmmaker Who Keeps Love Alive Through Her Art

I WAS INTRODUCED TO forty-seven-year-old Daphne Yeager-Ostendorf by a mutual friend at a film festival in New York City. After the screening, a group of us went down to a bar in the East Village and sat for a few hours to keep warm on the frigid winter night. Gary and I sat across from Daphne and quickly ended up deep in conversation with her about the movies we had seen and then about our own lives. She, too, was a filmmaker and was in preproduction on a large new personal project. She told me it was a documentary about her family. More specifically, it was about great loss. She explained, quite openly, that a few years ago her husband and nine-year-old daughter passed away. Now, she and her two children, Espen and Lilly, were retracing their steps and documenting their experience with the hope of helping others who were dealing with illness or the loss of a loved one.

The first words I could say were, "I'm so sorry." What I was really thinking was, *How incredible that you're able to talk about your loss so candidly, especially with two near strangers.* Death is often hidden away in modern-day society. Once the funeral is over, people usually expect the loved ones closest to the deceased to mourn quietly and then move on. And by move on, I mean forget. Perhaps talking about those who have passed makes people uncomfortable because there are few words of solace that can be offered. My meager "I'm sorry," for example. Many who have had someone close to them die end up omitting their loss from conversation in an attempt to make others more comfortable. I was so impressed by Daphne because she spoke about Olivia, her daughter, and Holger, her husband, with laughter in her voice. Pain too, of course. But I was struck by how unabashedly she recounted such a difficult time in her life and was able to do so with such poise. She didn't shut away her feelings or pretend like she hadn't suffered loss. Daphne managed to keep her loved ones with her and move forward at the same time, celebrating milestones with friends, spending time with her two children, and living her life in a way that I only hope I would be brave enough to do.

I thought about Daphne a great deal after our first meeting; however, we didn't meet again until six months later. Then, I talked to her about the book and how I was looking for people who had achieved balance in their lives. She marveled at how in line the book was with the film she was making. Daphne said that talking about her experience and creating art about what she went through helps her to process it and to heal.

Not too long after that I went to Daphne's apartment, a one-bedroom in Westchester County, New York, where she lived with her daughter and son. Money was tight and Daphne didn't have a car so they chose a small place near the train station, which enabled them all to get around with relative ease. We sat in her living room while her son closed the door to the bedroom to work on his college applications. With great difficulty, I began asking Daphne about the events that unfolded years ago and how she stays balanced after losing two of the most important people in her life.

IN 2006, DAPHNE, A WORLD TRAVELER much like Eric, was living with her German husband, Holger, and their three children in Milan, Italy. Holger, a schoolteacher, was on a student field trip to Poland when their youngest daughter, Olivia, only five years old at the time, started complaining about terrible headaches. Daphne took her to a clinic to get looked at. After being dismissed by the first doctor, Daphne, feeling like something was really wrong, went for a second opinion. They did an MRI and found a dark hole in the middle of her daughter's brain. Olivia had a tumor, five centimeters in diameter. It could be malignant or benign. They had no way of knowing without removing it.

Holger came back from Poland to care for the other kids while Daphne and Olivia traveled to a hospital in Munich, Germany, that specialized in neurological and pediatric care. She had lived in Germany previously so was fluent in the language. In fact, if you met Daphne on the streets of her hometown in California, you'd think she was born in Munich. Her accent is more German than American. Being familiar with the country was a blessing. There were so many decisions to make and so much responsibility on Daphne's shoulders, all of that with her husband back in Milan. And the news only got worse.

They discovered that Olivia had a tumor in the plexus of her brain. She underwent an eight-hour surgery to remove the mass. Anyone who has dealt with cancer knows there is a period of uncertainty after an operation like this. The family waited together for the results that would change their lives. And then the diagnosis came. They learned that, yes, Olivia was sick. Daphne recalled, "We were all sitting in the hospital room and the news came, and I'll never forget this either because we were always singing Olivia songs. She liked Johnny Cash, liked the song 'Folsom Prison Blues.' We were singing this song in the hospital room and the doctor came in with this news and . . . it's just like someone takes the earth from out under you. Up until that point I didn't think she was going to have cancer. You know you're always on this hope. You'll push that hope to the very maximum and then you get the news and you're really surprised. But then you go with it. You have to say, 'Okay, what's the next step?'"

Hope is the theme that could really describe Olivia and Daphne's entire experience. The mother and daughter stayed in Germany for five months, Olivia in the hospital undergoing chemo and radiation and Daphne at the nearby Ronald McDonald house in Munich, a facility for families who need a place to stay and recharge while their children receive treatment far from home. Holger almost left his job to go be with them, but ultimately, for his own mental well-being, felt he should stay. Daphne told me, "That was good for him, and I agreed with that because I knew he had to do what he had to do. At the same time it left me more alone. It left me alone with a lot of responsibility with Olivia." Holger and their other two children remained in Italy while Olivia and Daphne created their own mini-world inside a hospital room.

When Daphne talked about Olivia going through treatment, she brightened. Instead of radiation or chemo, she talked about how silly the two of them would be together, joking about handsome doctors, learning to spell so that Olivia would be ready for school, and living as much of a normal life as they could from inside the hospital. Daphne said, "This everyday life, this often saved us."

At first, Daphne couldn't understand how other mothers did things like go furniture shopping while their child was waiting for a lung and heart transplant. Soon, however, she realized that these normal actions were what helped each and every one of them get through the difficult moments. She said, "It's like going shopping at the penny market or going for a walk, just the simplest of things just gave you so much energy and you appreciated them."

Whenever Olivia was able, they filled their time with the normal things any mother and child might do together. Especially school. Daphne became not just Olivia's mother and health advocate. She became her teacher. Olivia wanted desperately to learn. Even though Daphne didn't want to put undue pressure on her child, she went along with what Olivia wanted because she knew how important it was to occupy her with activities that were life affirming. "We just kept on doing these kind of normal things . . . even though it's kind of weird to put your kid under pressure to learn how to spell." She continued, "It also kind of took her away from the pain she was going through, too, so it was actually a good thing. As much as she could do, we would do."

Like Sungrai, Olivia and Daphne implemented distraction techniques to escape from the ever-present pain and uncertainty of their situation. When Olivia did chemo for a straight week and couldn't leave the hospital, they looked out the window at all the people at the beach. They were silly together and played games. Being so close to Olivia gave Daphne strength and enabled her to share incredible moments of beauty with her daughter. They helped each other stay positive. Holger, being so far away and only visiting for bursts of time, didn't have the same experience. Daphne told me, "I think that he suffered a lot because of this negativity or this, like, being super scared. I mean, we're all scared. I stayed hopeful because of Olivia. I was so lucky because I was so close to her. When you're so close to a kid like this, you can't not be hopeful. These children are giving you this love and they need you."

Research on optimism is abundant in the world of science. In Daphne and Olivia's case, one benefit of their hopeful attitude in the face of cancer, surgeries, and hospitals was that it contributed to their emotional well-being and gave them increased coping skills during a very stressful time. In addition to their optimism, jokes and laughter (a language they were fluent in during hard times) have been shown to decrease pain and help people during times of great stress.

And there was hope to be had. After years in and out of hospitals, Olivia was getting better. She and Daphne were able to go back to Milan, receiving some care at the local hospital and only traveling back to Munich for occasional treatments. Finally, the news came that Olivia's scans were clear and showed no signs of cancer. Not remission, but still, no cancer. They could all breathe again.

It was then, when they were finally safe, even just for a moment, that tragedy struck the family. Holger kissed Daphne good-bye one day, told the kids to clean up their things, and left the house to play badminton. Daphne told me, "We thought, *Okay, everything is going to be okay,* and that's when Holger fell. That's when he was just playing badminton and collapsed from cardiac arrest."

At the very same moment that Holger died, Daphne, in the middle of an evening jog, stopped in front of a church to say a prayer for her family, asking for everyone in her family to be kept safe. When she returned home, an upstairs neighbor told her the news.

Daphne recalled, "I just went into shock . . . I felt really unbelievably sad but at the same time I have three children." She told them each in turn, having her heart break all over again each time she explained to one of her children that their father was gone. Daphne knew that the four of them couldn't heal by themselves. Daphne started attending emergency therapy twice a week to process her emotions.

Sitting there with Daphne during the interview, I had to fight all my natural impulses that were telling me to stop talking. Leave her alone. That it was wrong to ask her to recount all of these difficult times in her life. She was sitting there in front of me, of course affected by her story, but not breaking down. There were no tears. A few years have passed. Tears still come, but not with the same frequency. Daphne, a woman who finds comfort in talking with others, isn't upset when people ask questions. It's when people ask her to stop talking, to hide her loss, to not bring up Holger and Olivia, that she has trouble. Death, something that happens to all of us, is still a taboo subject. Daphne refuses to follow the unspoken rule that the dead should not be discussed. I kept going, asking her questions, knowing that the only one uncomfortable in the room was me.

If I think of my own death, my body barely reacts at all. I don't fear it. Concerns tend to be more practical. *Will my cats be okay? How would my family and friends handle the news?* When I even think about the idea of losing Gary, the distress I feel is physical. I turn hot, my heart races, and anxiety pulses through my body. How does one continue through life when the very future they had expected and desired has been upended? I asked Daphne what helped her to get through this next stage, processing her husband's death and then, ultimately, moving forward without him. She told me she relied heavily on the kindness of those around her who offered her love and support. Friends brought over food, helped by being good listeners, and took the children for outings to give Daphne much-needed breaks. She described their kindnesses as "stepping on little lily pads of love all the time."

She said, "It's not just all me and how I am. I feel it's really how my environment is with people who are very loving. So that really helped me—people who asked me at the right moment, you know, 'Are you okay?' and 'How's it going?' and they're like cheering for you." Hugs were also some of the best therapy that Daphne received. She said, "People were giving me hugs and like, not just normal hugs, like really holding me hugs." Daphne recalled being at the hospital during Olivia's illness. She told me, "There was a woman in the hallway one day. She saw me also suffering and just said, 'Honey, you just need a hug' and just came over and I thought, *Ah, she saved me again.* I get saved all the time just by hugs. I'm so corny but there really is something special and it's easy to do."

Researcher Jürgen Sandkühler from the University of Vienna released a study showing that when hugs are shared between two people who trust each other, the health and mental well-being benefits can be healing.[31] The study showed that the simple act of hugging can help reduce stress, fear, and anxiety, and can actually help lower one's blood pressure. This is all thanks to the release of a hormone called oxytocin. Oxytocin, also distributed through the body during childbirth and breastfeeding, is sometimes called the "bonding hormone." All of this from one action that takes only seconds.

Not everyone in her life reacted by giving hugs or bringing over food. As many who have lost someone important to them know, a percentage of people, even those we might consider the closest to us, may disappear rather than lend their support. Perhaps they don't know what to say or how to act. Daphne told me, "When people are in this situation, there is a tendency I think . . . everyone gets scared and sometimes jerk back. They don't want to get close to you. They're even hurting that you're hurting." In the years since Holger and Olivia died, Daphne has lost friends and made new friends. She said, "Sometimes I feel that a lot of people are afraid. They are so afraid that they really take distance, even my closest friends. I've lost a lot of friends now because they couldn't handle this or they want me to move on. I've maybe also alienated myself from them, too, because they are not fitting what I need. I'm different now after this happened."

The new friendships that Daphne has formed are based on her new identity. The people in her life aren't afraid of what she has been through. They don't look to quiet her when she talks about Holger and Olivia. Just the opposite. They talk about them too. Death is not a dirty word in her house. Neither is illness. It's a part of life, one that we all face in our own time and, hopefully, help each other through. Having those exceptional people in her life has aided her in profound ways. As Daphne noted, being there for someone in pain is one of the easiest things to do. It doesn't require much. A hug, a supportive word, a listening ear, a meal—anything that showed she was not alone.

DAPHNE AND HER CHILDREN had the summer to try to heal after Holger's death. Then, in the fall, Olivia's cancer came back and the cycle started all over again. She had chemo, lost her hair, couldn't sleep, and again Daphne had to try to stay positive in a difficult situation. This time, it was even more challenging. Daphne didn't have Holger to help her with Espen and Lilly or the emotional support of a spouse with whom to discuss Olivia's medical needs. She was still healing after his very sudden death. Previously, she had been able to just focus on Olivia without worrying about who was feeding or caring for her other children. Now as a single parent, she had to rely on friends who stepped up to help them while Daphne again traveled back and forth between Milan and Munich for Olivia's care.

Over the next two years, Olivia's health went through extremes. There were times the doctors thought she wouldn't make it, and then she would rebound. They would celebrate during the good times, fitting in as much living as they could. As strong as Olivia was, her body could not go on forever. Daphne told me, "There came a time where she just got sicker and sicker, and the doctor said she wouldn't make it anymore."

When Olivia was in her final stages of life, Daphne decided that she would take over her care. They left Milan for a visit to America. Daphne explained, "I wanted to go back to where I come from, Trinidad in California. But our plane was canceled. We ended up in Las Vegas and went from there and ended up in Zion National Park." As a family of four, they drove through the park, taking in the exquisite natural setting. They thought Olivia would die on that trip, she was in such bad shape. But once again, her little body pulled itself from the depths. Daphne said, "One minute you think she's on her deathbed and then she'd say, 'Okay, well, I'm hungry for ice cream.' You have to stop your sadness and be flexible, thinking, *Okay, let's just live now. She's good now. Let's go for it.*"

After that final trip, Daphne and her children returned to Milan where she acted as a nurse for Olivia. Doctors and nurses were in contact daily by phone and helped her keep Olivia comfortable. Still, at the same time, a lot of Daphne's friends disappeared. She said that when it became clear that Olivia was terminal, many who had been supportive in the past withdrew. They no longer knew what to say or how to help when all hope had been erased.

Olivia passed away at nine years old. She had been fighting cancer for almost half of her young life. When her daughter finally died, Daphne, as she explained it, went into shock for about nine months.

In some ways, years later, she says she's still in shock. Those four years of Olivia's illness were nonstop. With Olivia needing constant care and two healthy children to take care of, Daphne hadn't been able to fully process Holger's death. Perhaps none of them had. Holger died suddenly. Daphne had no time to say good-bye. She explained, "With Olivia I had the chance to say good-bye a thousand times and to give her tons of love and hold her and be with her." A certain amount of peace came with that kind of separation. With Holger, the emotions weren't as simple. Daphne felt frustrated that he hadn't had his heart checked sooner. The day before he collapsed, the two of them had been in the hospital with Olivia and Daphne had suggested that, since they were there, he have his heart looked at. Because they were in the pediatric wing, he dismissed the idea but said he would do it in the near future. Like so many of us, and especially those who act as caregivers, he postponed his own needs to focus on those of others. Knowing that Holger's death potentially could have been prevented evokes mixed feelings from Daphne. She allows herself to be upset with him, to feel love for him, whatever her mind and body need at that moment. She said the best thing she could do for herself was not to hold back what she felt inside. "If it's an anger part, a love part . . . just let it out. I think that keeps you clean somehow. . . . And it's important not to judge yourself for that part."

It's this ability to let out her emotions that drew me to Daphne. Her feelings aren't hidden away, only to be taken out when she's alone. She shares them. She talks about them with staggering honesty. Daphne told me, "The more you hide and the more you try to pretend things are okay, the worse it gets." She went on to explain that she gets frustrated when people say, "I'm fine" when they are really suffering inside. She believes a lot of people's problems could be greatly reduced just by opening up to others. Talking helps unload a bit of the emotional burden, to gain other perspectives, and, as Daphne noted, "It also gives people the opportunity to help."

WHEN DAPHNE CAME OUT OF HER FOG, she decided to come back home to the United States to study film. She wanted to make a documentary about what she and her family went through to help others going through similar experiences. She believes that there are far too many voices left unheard, that illness and death sections people off from the rest of society in a way that's unfair and that makes life even more difficult. Daphne explained, "I left people behind, not just Olivia and Holger. The people who have cancer. The kids. I always feel like they are voices not heard, really, especially kids in the stages that Olivia went through. It's like we lived in two different worlds. The cancer world and the real world, and I always wanted them somehow to be a little bit closer together so it would make our world a happier world, you know, not that we're like freaks out in this cancer land."

Daphne doesn't think there is one right way to get through the kind of tragedy her family faced. She is, however, proud of how her family did it, how they supported Olivia and supported one another. Daphne said about the film, "I think that's one of the motivations. I always felt like it would be good also to help these people. It's not to show what we're doing and what we did. It's not like the recipe to how things are going to be, but it's like how we did it and maybe people can get strength to just see how we did it and how Olivia did it."

Over the summer in 2013, Daphne, Espen, and Lilly traveled back to Zion National Park. Money was tight so they camped along their journey, a drive across the country to visit the places they had gone on their last trip with Olivia. They visited the cinema where they saw a film together and the hotel where the three kids made a funny video. While therapeutic, it was also a very emotional road trip. Daphne said, "This trip wasn't a vacation really. It was also to say we were there, and it's different now."

Being gone in a physical sense doesn't mean Olivia and Holger are erased from her life. Daphne finds that by talking to them, she keeps them close. She also makes sure to recall past experiences with Espen and Lilly to keep those memories from their childhoods alive, the moments when it was the five of them rather than three. Moving forward as this smaller, different family doesn't mean leaving Holger and Olivia behind. Daphne said it's really important to keep them "always a little bit alive" just by talking about them. She went on to say, "Because in the world when a kid dies, nobody wants to say their name anymore. It's terrible."

TALKING TO OTHERS ABOUT HER EXPERIENCE, spending time with her children, and making art are just a few of the ways that Daphne has found healing. Another method, one that she used throughout Olivia's illness and continues to use today, is to stay active. Daphne would run to release some of her excess stress. As many caretakers know, it's not always possible to take a lot of personal time. In Munich during chemo, rather than running, Daphne would enlist the other moms who were there with their sick children to join her for a bit of exercise. She said, "I would get the moms out and say, 'Let's go walk around the hospital.' At nighttime, we would do our rounds at like twelve at night and laugh and talk about guys."

Daphne had to stop running recently when she hurt her back. Now, she cycles. Anything to keep her body moving. Dealing with death and the ups and downs of illness is hard on the mind and on the body. Daphne said that it was vital to her to "let that bad part out, that steam" by working out in some fashion.

As a mother responsible for so much over the years, running or cycling also serves as a time when Daphne can be alone, doing something that's just for her. Research about people who act as caregivers shows that taking time to care for oneself is vital to personal health and long-term mental well-being. Because caretaking, especially for someone who needs round-the-clock care like Olivia did, can be physically demanding, isolating, and stressful, it can do a great deal of damage to the body. Working out, making time for friends, eating a balanced diet, and getting a rest from caretaking duties helps both the caretaker and the person being cared for.

Equally important for Daphne has been finding joy in her work. When she moved to White Plains, New York, nearly a year after Olivia died, Daphne entered a graduate program for documentary film. That's when she began exploring her own story through her art. However, there were practical things to consider when she went back to school. Holger's pension doesn't provide Daphne and her children enough money to live on. In addition to being a single parent working on a large-scale personal project, Daphne finds fulfillment in paying jobs that utilize her film skills.

She did emphasize that focusing too much on work can be problematic. She finds that some people use work as an escape after a traumatic experience. Daphne told me, "I've worked really hard;

actually it's crazy but it's good. If I didn't have that . . . I wouldn't be how I am now. On the other hand, it's also dangerous because a lot of people who just delve into work and stuff, they just brush over really what they should be working on. So you've got to have a balance, a really big balance, and you don't have the answers. The balance is always different . . . You always have to step back from yourself a little bit and say, 'Hey, what do I really need now? Am I doing too much or too little? Am I too stressed?'"

Balancing all of Daphne's different responsibilities and interests, as well as tending to her emotional state, requires constant reflection. This ability to look inward, similar to Michal's display of emotional intelligence, enables Daphne to adjust her life and her schedule depending on her current needs. What she was able to do the first year after Olivia passed is different from where she is now. By listening to herself, she makes sure that she keeps on top of what she needs to be doing for her family, for her work, and for her emotional health.

SEEING DEATH FROM THE PERSPECTIVE of a young wife and mother has changed the way Daphne looks at life. She doesn't want to live in her past sorrows. She wants to experience as much joy as possible. She knows, better than most, that there is no guarantee she will get to see tomorrow. That makes today so much more important. Daphne knows that Olivia and Holger would want her to keep living and enjoying the time she has, even without them. Daphne explained about Olivia, "She would just say, 'Momma do it, you know, have fun. You can have fun. I would.'" She went on to say, "If I had died and she would be alive, I would always be going, *Come on you guys, do whatever you want to do to be happy.* It's about that. It's not about pleasing anyone or having anything; just be happy."

Being happy when you've just lost the person you love is easier said than done. It requires accepting a life different from the one you had. A new one must be made. As Daphne noted about her trip back to Zion with Espen and Lilly, they are a different family now than they were when Olivia and Holger were alive. She said, "It's not like how it was. It's really weird. It's like really, someone took your life and broke it and then you've got to put things together. And it's not the way it was at all. That's what I'm learning now. I feel it's easier going when I realize, *Okay, these are fragments of something very new,* not compare it so much to how it was with Holger and Olivia." She continued, "We love them. We love them like crazy and that doesn't change and we're going to keep thinking about them every day and love them, but this is what we have in our little family right now. Let's see how we move on."

Life may not be what it was before Olivia's illness and before Holger died. That doesn't stop Daphne from knowing at this moment just how lucky she is. She's grateful for the life she has. Daphne said that because of her and her children's history, "We know it could go any minute. We've seen two cases where life changes like that, so there's a lot of gratitude. We know it could be a lot worse." She continued, "I'm happy even if I hurt my back and I don't care. I can still walk. It makes you super appreciative."

Being grateful for what they do have, rather than resentful about what they lost, aids them in moving forward. They are not leaving Holger and Olivia behind. They remain with Daphne and the kids at all times. Knowing how quickly everything can disappear inspires them to, as cliché as it sounds, live their lives to the fullest. Carpe diem, as they say. Seize the day. And Daphne does. She relishes her time with her kids, with her friends, with her art. She laughs often and freely.

A MONTH OR SO AFTER MEETING WITH DAPHNE, Gary and I were celebrating my thirty-second birthday at Pure Food and Wine in New York City. The place was packed, so our little romantic table was set right next to another table. Around the time we got to dessert, Gary and I started chatting with the other couple. They told us about their daughter and how they were visiting New York City from Pennsylvania. We told them a bit about ourselves. Then, as we asked about their other children, the husband told us that their son had died in Iraq. They, like Daphne, worked to help other families who had faced loss. And by helping, they were healing.

Over the years I've read numerous stories about people who have gone through trauma and then, instead of trying to erase it from their history, they do their best to help others who are going through similar events. They know how hard it is and want to ease that burden by sharing their story. That's what Daphne is doing by participating in this book and by making her film. She wants to rebuild her own life into something new. It doesn't happen overnight, but it does happen. Emery and Daphne are living proof of it—that humans can move forward after suffering loss, showing great resilience. For Daphne, it took the love of her children and powerful friendships to help her heal. She only hopes she can offer the same type of healing support for others.

FINDING BALANCE THROUGH RELIGION AND SPIRITUALITY

•

How can we find the positive
even under negative circumstances?

"I'll have friends sometimes ask, 'Why do you go to church on Sunday?' The reality of it is that Sunday prepares me for Monday and Tuesday and Wednesday and Thursday and Friday. I don't go to church on Sunday because I think that God is going to punish me if I don't. I go to church on Sunday so I can be reminded that I need to be good on Monday."

—*Alex*

chapter 9

Alex,

*an Alternative Healer Who Lives
a Life of Body, Mind, and Spirit*

WHEN I WAS TWENTY-FIVE, something went terribly wrong with my feet. What started out as a little discomfort turned into crippling pain that left me barely able to walk. I needed to drive or use a wheelchair for any distance longer than a block or two. I went to doctor after doctor after doctor. In fact, over a five-year period, I probably saw nearly fifteen different podiatrists, neurologists, orthopedists, and physiatrists in small offices and huge hospitals. I had X-rays and MRIs as well as experimental treatments and physical therapy. No one knew what was wrong. No one could help. I thought I would live my entire life feeling pain with every single step. That was, until Gary's cousin told us about the miracle man who had helped her when traditional doctors didn't have a clue.

His name was Alex, and he traveled the United States treating professional athletes for their injuries. His background was in Chinese medicine and massage therapy, two methods of healing he had combined to perfect his own brand of hands-on therapy. Gary's cousin told me he treated top athletes (mostly in the National Football League), keeping them healthy as they faced injury after injury on the field. (A top athlete I was not.) Still, I was skeptical. No one else had been able to make any difference. What would he know that the other doctors didn't? Plus, because Alex was always on the move, we would have to travel to Utah to see him. We were broke at the time. The roof on our newly bought house had gone bust. Flying from New York to Utah to stay in a hotel for a few days would make a significant dent in our already dwindling bank accounts. But Gary was adamant. "This could be something," he said. "This could change everything." He believed. After five years of disappointment, I no longer did.

That first day in Utah, Alex didn't have his hands on my feet for more than a few seconds before he knew what was wrong. Scar tissue. He said my feet were riddled with it. What should have been healthy tissue had turned hard and knotted, so it felt as if I had jagged gravel wedged between the skin and bone. He had seen it before in NFL players, but it was always worked out before it got too bad. Mine was like an infestation. And yet, having Alex declare what was wrong was some of the best news I had ever heard. I finally had a diagnosis that made sense and, even better, a game plan to start healing. For three days, totally pro bono, Alex came to the hotel for a few hours in the morning and few hours at night to work the scar tissue out of my feet and to teach Gary his techniques. I was finally on the road to recovery. I wasn't rich. I wasn't famous. I wasn't a top-tier NFL player, and yet Alex gave me his time and his expertise because he genuinely wants people to get better. He has a gift for understanding the body, especially soft tissue, and wants to share his knowledge with others so they can heal and go back to living their lives without pain.

For six months after our trip to Utah, Gary worked on my feet the way Alex had taught him, putting his acting career on hold and dedicating his free time to my care. It's now a year and a half later and I would estimate my feet are 80 percent better. (I'm still working my way up to 100 percent.) My wheelchair sits unused down in the basement, and I have walked a record two miles all by myself. My life has changed forever, and it's thanks to Alex.

Now, I wouldn't have chosen Alex for this book had he just healed me. That gets him my eternal gratitude, like the surgeon who removed my thyroid cancer. For this book I was looking for more than those who had shown compassion. I was searching for people who also had inner peace, control, balance. During those days in Utah and after, as he continued my treatment from afar, I witnessed Alex's spirit, his kindness, and his positivity, all of which were extraordinary.

He doesn't just exhibit these qualities in his healing; they're at the very core of who he is. If I could use one word to describe it, I would choose "love." As much as Alex healed me with his knowledge and his hands, I would say his love for me and others is just as responsible for my brand-new life and for his gift to mend the injured.

LOOKING AT ALEX'S STORY, I think there have always been three constants in his life. Starting with his earliest years, it was religion—his faith in God. Then, as he entered his twenties, he found his calling in sports therapy and Chinese medicine, and then as a husband and father. I would guess that over 90 percent of Alex's energy and interests fall into one of those three categories. Certainly that's where his time goes. If he's not working with injured athletes, he's likely doing something with his wife, Alicia, with their five children, or with his church. Of the three passions, there is one that influences everything he does: his faith in God.

Some of the people I have interviewed for this book identified themselves as spiritual, some as atheists, and some didn't talk about that area of their lives. It is obvious that religion is absolutely pivotal to Alex. It shapes who he is as a person and how he maintains a balanced and peaceful life.

As a lifelong member of the Church of Jesus Christ of Latter-Day Saints (commonly called the Mormon Church), Alex maintains a powerful relationship with God. He said his faith helps him with his work, his marriage, his family, and, of course, his own sense of well-being. He told me, "I try to have a great relationship with God. You know I say my personal prayers and communicate with him every day. My prayers are always about letting me be kind, letting me be thoughtful, letting me be slow to anger, letting me be helpful, you know, letting those people who I put my hands on today feel the difference; letting them feel better when they leave." To me, the qualities that Alex seeks in his prayers lay the foundation for living a balanced and meaningful life. His prayers help him focus on the things that truly matter and to mirror the behaviors of his greatest teacher. Alex explained, "Jesus Christ is very important to me, he's important to my kids. He's a very central figure in our home, so we try to pattern our day and our life based on the things that Jesus teaches."

BEING KIND, THOUGHTFUL, PATIENT, and helpful—these are the characteristics that Alex strives to perfect, and all of them are key to staying balanced in any situation. Staying calm and kind is easy when things are going well. It's how we react under less favorable circumstances that really shows how far we've come and how far we still have to go. So how does Alex handle negative situations? What do his daily prayers and belief in God enable him to do?

For a start, his faith and outlook on life give him the power to see something good in every bad situation. He said, "There are positives to every negative, and I've learned through the course of my life through many negative situations to look for the positive in those. That's really allowed me to have a peace and a comfort that I didn't have when I was a lot younger and didn't have that figured out."

One particular example of turning a negative into a positive came early in Alex's career. He was at a conference presenting to a roomful of doctors about nutrition and herbology. Now, this was at a time when alternative medicine was seen as a pretty far-out idea and the people who practiced it were viewed as wacky. Early on in the talk one man stood up and said, "You realize that what you're talking about is just sheer voodoo." Alex told me, "So my first thought process was almost to attack back, but as I thought about how to make this a positive experience, I thought, *Don't take offense,* so I simply said, 'What is it that you feel you're going to be getting out of my lecture today?' And he was like, 'Absolutely nothing. I just came because I wanted to tell you that I think you're voodoo medicine.' I said, 'Do you feel better?' and he said, 'I don't feel anything.' And I said, 'Okay, then I hope you have a wonderful day.'"

That was it. The man stood up and left. What happened next was the gold. The other doctors in the room marveled at how calm Alex had been in the face of someone coming to his lecture for the sole purpose of being rude. Alex knew that nothing he could have said in that moment would change the man's mind, so instead of defending himself or getting into an argument, he let the man say his piece and then leave. From that moment on, the lecture was no longer about herbology and nutrition. That one negative moment sparked a discussion on how important it is for doctors to learn how to work cooperatively with people like Alex. He told them, "At some point in time you're going to have patients who are seeing people like me, so for no other reason you should simply learn to understand this. You may not believe in it, you may not want to do it with your patients, but you should simply learn to at least understand it."

His presentation then turned into an open forum on how the two types of medicine could work together. To this day, Alex still keeps in touch with a few of the doctors who were in that room. Some of them even incorporate alternative medicine into their practice now. And it all began with one negative voice. I look at that situation and think back to the qualities that Alex prays for. Kindness? Check. Thoughtfulness? Check. Patience? Double-check. And of course helping others.

Alex's faith doesn't just tell him to be kind to the people who agree with him. His belief demands that he be kind to everyone he meets, even if they hold drastically different views from his own. He said, "It's easy, I think, in religion to sometimes get caught up in what you feel is the goodness of religion. What my faith has taught me is that regardless of how I morally feel about something, I can tolerate a belief that somebody else has rather than come out and make them feel, or try to make them feel bad, or try to, in the words of religion, make them 'see the light.' That's never really made a lot of sense to me."

Rather than pushing his personal beliefs and morals on others, Alex strives to make everyone he meets feel welcome. He called upon a Maya Angelou quote to further explain how he feels: "People will forget what you said. People will forget what you did. But people will never forget how you made them feel," said Angelou. "I think that tolerance is that way," explained Alex. "It's a feeling—so I don't have to believe necessarily in the same things somebody else does, and somebody else doesn't have to believe in the way that I believe. But certainly, I can be tolerant of their belief and help them feel comfortable and loved when they're with me. That's what Jesus taught me."

Alex greets everyone he meets with a hug and a smile, and no one is made to feel judged or looked down upon. I think that's an especially valuable lesson in a world where so many different groups of people hold opposing beliefs. We don't always have to agree, but we can always be kind. And if someone is unkind, we always have the power to walk away.

It takes an enormous amount of self-control to not react with anger or judgment, especially when someone does or says something cruel. This is a quality the ten people I've spoken with have in spades. Whether it's discussing a difficult topic with a spouse or friend, or being on the receiving end of rudeness from a complete stranger, the people I've had the privilege of spending time with for this book don't seem to aspire to win or to be right. They strive for open communication and understanding. For them, being kind and tolerant isn't just lip service.

Alex said that praying every day reminds him that he should always uphold those qualities that are so important to him, the ones that allow him to be the person he wants to be even when life gets bumpy. In addition to saying his personal prayers, Alex also attends church with his family every Sunday. "We aren't just Sabbath-day members. I mean, we really try to live our faith seven days a week," he said. "I'll have friends sometimes ask, 'Why do you go to church on Sunday?' The reality of it is that Sunday prepares me for Monday and Tuesday and Wednesday and Thursday and Friday. I don't go to church on Sunday because I think that God is going to punish me if I don't. I go to church on Sunday so I can be reminded that I need to be good on Monday."

Alex said that church isn't just about reaffirming his best qualities each week, though it certainly does do that. It also gives him an enormous sense of community. As many people know, moving to a new place can be tough. In the summer of 2013, Alex and his family relocated to Massachusetts from Utah. His only previous experience with living on the East Coast was during his mission experience in Washington, DC, back when he was nineteen. (Many Mormons opt to serve a two-year mission around that age.) His friends back west warned him about those East Coasters: *They're rude. They're gruff. They're difficult to get to know.* But that wasn't Alex's experience at all. The moment he entered his local church, the congregation was ready and eager to welcome him and his family with open arms. They came over to help the new family unpack. They said, 'Don't worry about food this week,' and dropped off meals for his family to eat as they got settled in their new home. He told me about his new community, "You feel like they are family and they become family very quickly."

The benefits of religion aren't cut and dry in the eyes of the scientific world. Like all things, it depends on the religion, the way it's practiced, and how it's interpreted. Many agree that the benefits of attending a weekly service relate to being a part of a community. T. M. Luhrmann recently wrote in the *New York Times* how through her work as an anthropologist she's seen people who really did seem to look out for one another through sickness and personal strife.[32] And it's well documented that having a strong social support network of friends and family certainly is good for one's physical and mental health. She also notes in the article that attending a religious service regularly can boost the immune system and lower blood pressure. I've personally known people who were not religious who attended services just for the sense of community. In an ever-increasingly virtual world, being in a room with other people can be a powerful draw all by itself.

Now, as a happy atheist, I'm not envious of a person's faith in God. I interviewed atheists, spiritual people, and devout people for this book, all of whom have gotten to where they are through their different belief systems. But I'll freely admit, I'm positively jealous of Alex's instant community, the same way I feel about those who go to other churches, synagogues, mosques, and temples. A house of worship brings people with similar beliefs and values together. It isn't always easy to find people who share our values in this some-times isolating world. The beautiful thing about attending a religious service each week is that you get to see people who live near one another and share a common experience. It's the perfect setup to meet new people and create long-lasting friendships. That's some-thing that Alex knows very well. And it's not just for him. There is something for every person in his family. For example, he said his kids immediately met other children in the area through the youth services the church provided.

When challenges arise, Alex said he can always go back to the teachings of the church to be reminded of the behaviors he expects from himself. Religion gives Alex and his family so many things—a figure to model their behavior after in the form of Jesus Christ, a community to support and be supported by, shared values within their home, and a feeling of being loved at all times by God. Alex's prayers became a mantra for me: Be kind, be thoughtful, be slow to anger, and be helpful. From everything I've seen, Alex lives up to those prayers in the goals he sets for himself every day.

IN ADDITION TO A LIFELONG RELATIONSHIP with God, Alex has maintained a happy and loving marriage with his wife, Alicia. For more than twenty-seven years, they have raised a family and loved and supported each other. He repeated what Cathy's husband told me about her marriage—that in all their years together, he could count on one hand the number of fights they had. In Alex's case, he said this wasn't because they agreed on absolutely everything, but instead because before they tied the knot, they came up with a list of ways to maintain a happy life together.

Both Alex and Alicia came from divorced families, not a fate either of them wanted to repeat for themselves or for their children. Alex explained, "That was something we talked about—that divorce wasn't going to be an option in our life—so we talked about the things we needed to do to make sure we didn't reach that point. We came up with a plan and we've followed that plan and it's worked for us." Of course, I immediately wanted to know the details of their plan.

The first item: to always continue to court each other. That includes having a standing date night each week, leaving little love notes for each other, and being affectionate. Alex and Alicia didn't just want to hold hands and kiss for their own sakes. They also wanted

The National Marriage Project at the University of Virginia reviewed the social science literature on romantic relationships and analyzed data from a nationally representative survey of more than 1,600 married heterosexual couples between the ages of eighteen and fifty-five all to see what date night can really do for a marriage.[33] Authors W. Bradford Wilcox and Jeffrey Dew found that a regularly scheduled date night improves communication, commitment, and that sense of passion one tends to feel in the early stages of a relationship while also decreasing stress and introducing a sense of novelty to the marriage. Anyone who has been in a long-term relationship knows that habits tend to be formed. Date night allows a couple to step out of their regularly scheduled lives and to shake things up a bit.

their children to see that they had two parents who loved each other deeply. Alex said the kids joke that seeing their mom and dad kiss or find love notes is "gross," but Alex told me he knows they really get it. And he hopes that seeing two parents who love each other every day will show them what a positive relationship looks like.

If you'll remember, Emery and Elaine, with their sixty years of marriage, also maintained a similar relationship—one with kissing, hand holding, and public displays of affection. Cathy also talked about how important cuddling with her husband was for her morning routine to start her day off right. As I mentioned before, Gary and I have eight years of marriage under our belts, and we also cuddle, kiss, and hold hands each day. In the writing world, it would be equivalent to that age-old piece of advice to show, not tell. I say hold hands every day if you want your marriage to last forever. Alex and Alicia, Cathy and Michael, and Emery and Elaine (with their combined 120+ years of married experience) are perfect proof of that as a successful strategy for long-term marital bliss.

Another major item on Alex and Alicia's list was to always be selfless with each other and always put the other first. Alex said, "It's interesting because the more I would do for her, the more I wanted to do for her and vice versa. So what initially I thought would be work wasn't really hard work." What I love about this rule is that if both truly uphold this promise, they will always strive for a win-win solution. (Yes, I'm obsessed with win-win solutions.) If I'm thinking about Gary's happiness, and he's thinking about mine, it's likely we'll come to a solution that works for both of us. This way of living also prompts partners to look at something from the other person's point of view and ask, *What are his or her needs? Is there something I can do to help fulfill those needs?*

Kindness also made their list, as did gratitude. And, not surprisingly, communication is another important element in Alex and Alicia's marriage. Alex wasn't always successful at communicating with Alicia, but he learned fast. When he was growing up in California, his parents worked hard just to get by. As he got older, he often heard comments like, "Well, it's okay, Alex, that you're poor. You're Mexican." Or, "It's okay if you have welfare, 'cause, you know, you're Mexican." There are so many things wrong with those comments. They are racist, they made assumptions about Alex's capabilities and ambitions, and, of course, they lumped all people from Central and South America together. (Alex's parents came to the United States from Argentina.) Because of this bigotry, Alex admitted that he struggled with a bit of an ego problem as those wounds were healing. People expected so little of him that he felt he had something to prove. Ego can be one of the worst items to bring to a conflict because it makes us strive to be right rather than to come to a meaningful resolution.

Alex said his ego made it difficult to work through issues early in his marriage in the positive and constructive way he does now. He said, "If Alicia did something that was hurtful, rather than me telling her early on in a loving way that it was really hurtful, I would do something to hurt her back. But we got out of that really quick, like we figured it out really fast early on in our marriage and so then it was fine. We just learned that talking about it and being open about it and knowing that what we were talking about came from an area of love and . . . it became much easier not to take offense."

I was curious how Alex had changed since his youth when he was on the receiving end of those racist comments, and how he responds to criticism now. After all, that advice we all received when we were children—not to take things personally—can be easier said than done. Especially when the insults are as vile as the ones Alex heard. Alex explained that the key is to quiet one's ego with self-control, confidence, and the wherewithal not to emotionally invest oneself in the hurtful words of others. "I've grown really comfortable in my own skin," he said. "So when someone says something negative to me, I know better. I just know what they're saying isn't true; therefore, I don't feel I need to validate what they are saying because I know *me*. I know how I think. I know how I feel. I know how I behave. And so, I get that their perception of me is their reality, and I let them have their reality. I think, *If you want to think I'm the biggest jerk in the world or I'm a charlatan or I'm a fake or whatever it is, you have that right. And if you want to live in that space, go ahead.* So I don't take on people's negative emotions about me. It just doesn't negatively impact me because I simply won't allow it."

Alex really does shrug off insults. Using a less hurtful scenario than the racist comments from his past, Alex told me that if, for example, someone tells him they hate his shirt, to him, that just means the offending party wouldn't wear it. It's a shirt *he* likes. He's confident wearing it so other people's opinions are irrelevant. It's how he feels about himself that matters. Now, if a close friend or family member came to him with an issue, that would be a different matter. He'd listen and talk it out and adjust his behavior if it was called for, just as he does in his marriage. If someone is just out to be hurtful or says things that Alex knows to be untrue, he ignores them. He's confident enough in who he is to discern between truth and fiction. I loved what he said about allowing other people to have their own reality. If they think he's a jerk, that's fine. They are allowed to think whatever they like. It doesn't take anything away from him and it doesn't make it true.

ALEX'S REACTION TO CRITICISM isn't the only thing that has changed since his youth. He said that growing up in a family that struggled financially made him buy into the idea that happiness comes from monetary and material success. He explained, "Alicia grew up middle class. I grew up more low income. And so the idea of the American dream was, *I've got to have a great car and a great house and live in the right neighborhood and have my kids go to the right school.* That's how I had programmed myself to think of the American dream." And then, Alex achieved all of those things. His business was thriving, and he and his family were able to benefit financially from his achievements. As he came face to face with what he had always perceived to be the ideal, he said his thoughts on what brings happiness changed drastically.

"We had good cars and we had a great house, and then we moved to a greater house and we did some traveling. And now that I'm older and I've got two grown kids, at the end of the day I've come to the conclusion that happiness and peace and comfort and tranquility all revolve around love and not around things. And so having a big house, a nice car, living in a great neighborhood or in a great school district really didn't provide me with anything of great value. What has provided me great value is the love my wife has for me and the love that I have for her, the love that our children share with each other. When I see them communicate with each other . . . that brings me happiness."

Back in Utah, Alex lived in an 8,000-square-foot home. That's just over triple the size of the average American home. Even with five children to house and care for, that's a whole lot of space. Knowing what he knows now, he and his family took the opportunity to downsize when they moved to Massachusetts. Their new home is about 2,200 square feet, less than about one floor of their former home. Does Alex miss all the space he had back in Utah? Not really. He said that one of the most beautiful parts of downsizing has been spending more time together as a family. Back in Utah, Alex might have been in his office, Alicia in her office, and then one kid in the basement, another on the third floor in his room, and another in the family room. Isolated. Two of the kids are now off at college, so only five of them occupy the new house. They see one another right when they walk in the door. As a family, they are spending more time together than ever before. Alex told me that the night before our interview, his kids had a bunch of friends over for a movie night. In a 2,200-square-foot home, there is no escaping the sounds generated from a get-together like that. Alex noted, "It was loud, it was crazy, and it was fun."

He added, "They feel that we love them and their friends love them and that's what makes them happy." Not a big house. Not furniture or iPods or purses. Love. Just like Sungrai's father learned that money wasn't what made him happy, so did Alex.

As I mentioned earlier, Alex has three main passions that make up the vast majority of his life. Faith, family, and his work as a sports therapist. It was actually during his two-year mission with his church to Washington, DC, that Alex discovered his interest in health care. When he wasn't talking to others about his faith, he was volunteering at Georgetown Medical Facility. Fluent in English and Spanish, Alex used his translation skills to help Spanish-speaking patients communicate with their doctors. It was then that he fell in love with health care, and the idea started brewing that he could spend his life helping people.

While working at an ornamental iron company, making decorative railings and such, Alex started taking classes in massage therapy. Soon after, Alicia's father was diagnosed with squamous cell carcinoma, a life-changing moment that prompted Alex to seriously pursue a future in alternative medicine. He explained, "They just really butchered his care. It wasn't a positive experience for our family.

He was misdiagnosed initially and then it turned out to be malignant when they told me it was benign. So through that experience I thought there's got to be something that's better because there were really no real answers then."

Alex enrolled in a master's program in Chinese medicine, determined to learn alternative methods to help those who had been failed by the kind of traditional care his father-in-law had gone through. He said, "I really read about Chinese medicine and I fell in love with it. I thought that I could really go do things in internal medicine with it and really help people from this integrative approach."

Alex continued doing massage to pay his way through school and found that more and more professional athletes, like members of the Oakland Raiders, came in looking for his services. His supervisor, noticing all these pro players who would come in and ask for Alex by name, suggested that he pursue sports medicine. And so he did. By combining his background in massage therapy with his education in Chinese medicine, Alex created his own brand of treatment. He told me, "I developed a technique to change negative muscle memory patterns in a fairly quick way. And the more I practiced, the better I got at it and the faster the results were. And fortunately for me it worked and here I am twenty years later and still really enjoying what I do."

Like all the other people in this book, Alex is passionate about his work. And yet, when I spoke to him, I noticed another common theme throughout the interviews. Even though Alex found what he was called to do for a living, and did so quite early on, it took him years to figure out how to balance his work and his personal life. Alex, like Leanne, had dedicated too much of himself to his work for a long time. If someone called with an injury or an issue, he'd be there. He also saw student athletes for free for many years, and as word spread, his client list grew and grew. Toward the end of his time in California, about two thousand patients a month were coming to his practice.

He told me, "I ended up getting burned out. It got to the point where I didn't know how to say no and I wasn't very good at that time at trying to find a balance between work, family, friends, myself. And so, it's interesting, there's a difficult balance when you are a health care provider and you feel that there is a calling for you in that, to put boundaries. I just never put boundaries on myself, so when someone would call and they were hurt, I felt compelled to go help them. I never really felt that it was a negative thing for me, but I got tired. I just got burned out. I wasn't unhappy. I was just tired."

He left his practice in California to his partner (his brother) and started working just with elite athletes for a number of years. He would travel during the week and spend weekends at home with his family in Utah. It worked for a while. Alex was able to travel, meet with his athletes, and then have time off to rest or see a movie while the athletes practiced. But ultimately, he didn't want to limit the time he spent with his wife and kids to just the weekends. That's when he opened up his new facility in Massachusetts. He gets to work with his elite athletes—high school and college kids as well as weekend warriors (his words)—and go home each night to see his family. He no longer allows his schedule to get so filled up like he did back in California, and he is able to sleep in his own bed each night. Instead of feeling tired, he said he is energized and able to have all the things in his life that bring him joy. Nothing was sacrificed.

So many people I meet—writers, filmmakers, visual artists, activists—are searching for a way to do what they love full time, and they believe that if they could just find that one job, balance and happiness will surely come. I've been guilty of the same trap, that belief that emotional balance and well-being comes from being in a great relationship, having a dream job, or living in the right house. It certainly is an improvement from being in a bad relationship and hating a job or living in a house that's crumbling, but these aren't the only factors that make up a good life. Leanne was doing what she wanted. So was Alex. And yet, because they gave so much of themselves to their work, their balance was off. If they were trying to be a cake, they had all the right ingredients but their measurements were out of whack. That makes for a dry, yucky baked good—or in their cases, some very tired, overworked people. Leanne wasn't her best self until she asked herself what she needed outside of her work. Alex was burned out until he was able to set boundaries between him and his patients. Once both of them were able to take the time they needed for themselves, they became better for the work they were doing.

BEING IN THE SPORTS WORLD, Alex knows how to take care of himself. With regular physical activity and a diet comprised of mostly organic and whole foods, Alex strives to treat his body as kindly as he can. When Alex works with his athletes, he won't just stand on the sidelines watching them sweat; he'll take part in the exercises. He loves being outside so he enjoys mountain biking, playing tennis and basketball, and running alongside his athletes.

Alex said about the importance of exercise, "I believe that the body is very connected physically, spiritually, and emotionally. I don't think there is a way to separate those." Leanne, Zoe, Emery, Eric, Cathy, Michal, and Daphne would all agree. During each interview, I asked the question about exercise and in turn heard almost everyone say just how good they feel when they work out and how not working out causes them imbalance. Same with eating. Emery prided himself on all the fresh fruits and vegetables he eats. Zoe and Leanne eat according to their ethics as well as to enhance their health with a totally plant-based diet. Food is something to enjoy. It's also something to fuel our bodies so we're capable of doing all the things we want to do. If I ate a cupcake in the morning and then asked my body to run a marathon, it might just laugh at me. If I ate a spinach, mango, blackberry, walnut, and lemon smoothie (my breakfast this morning), I would have a lot more power to make it through whatever task I ask of my body.

I'm not going to cite a study here, mostly because there are too many to count. But if you look at the news, or in any health magazine, or talk to your doctor, you'll find that a diet rich in fruits and vegetables and low in saturated fats will give you more energy and reduce your risk for heart disease, stroke, high blood pressure, type 2 diabetes, obesity, cancer, and more. When people ask, "Is there a magic pill that can make me healthy?" I say we take our magic pills every day during breakfast, lunch, and dinner. It's called *food*, and it's supposed to aid our bodies and our health, not bring upon illness, early death, and bad moods. Yes, eating a healthy diet can even improve our mental health. The same with regular workouts. The benefits are incalculable.

Alex also agrees with everyone else in the book that nature is a positive force in his life. Not the type to naturally notice the little things in the great outdoors, Alex said that he has found the capacity to take pleasure in nature for its simplicity through his relationship with Alicia. He said, "Alicia will stop and she'll look at a leaf and she'll be like, 'Ah Alex, oh my gosh, come on and look at this leaf' and I'm like, 'Look at a leaf? You stopped the bike to go look at a leaf?'" He learned to appreciate this trait in Alicia and cherishes the things she has prompted him to see that he otherwise would have missed. "All of a sudden you'll just hear this song of birds, which typically isn't something that I'd really pick up on—which is why I so enjoy doing things with her. She has taught me to enjoy, to stop and smell the roses. It's just so beautiful and just breathtaking and so peaceful to hear the running brooks and to hear the wind blow the leaves, the aspens; it's just beautiful."

As the people in this book emphasize, whether it's mountains, the ocean, a tiny patch of dirt with a caterpillar or a forest, the smells, sounds, and miraculous views supplied by the great outdoors can relax us and make us feel one of the best sensations a human being can experience: awe.

KNOWING ALEX HAS BEEN A PERSONAL PRIVILEGE. After all, he's the man who gave me my feet back and a life without constant pain. Before sitting down for the interview, I knew him a little bit. During my treatments, we talked about his family and about his work with athletes. I shared a bit about myself. From our time together, I felt I knew his spirit, that he was the kind of person whom anyone would be lucky to have in their lives. Interviewing him not only confirmed my beliefs. It also enhanced them. When he says that love is what guides him through everything, I believe him.

Some people just ooze a certain quality. It could be good. It could be bad. Alex oozes love. He genuinely seems to want the best for everyone he meets and to help create positivity in whatever way he can. All the goodness he takes in for himself through his faith, family, and profession, he gives right back to the world. Love, kindness, and generosity are all qualities to be shared. Just being in the room with Alex gives me those feelings that I can then take and pass on to others. When I think of him, I go back to that Maya Angelou quote: "People will forget what you said. People will forget what you did. But people will never forget how you made them feel." If I can take the way Alex makes me feel, that sense of acceptance and camaraderie, and pass that on to others, I'll be well on my way to living a very good life.

LIVING
OUR DREAMS

·

Is it possible to "have it all"
and still live a happy life
rich in integrity and balance?

"A lot of it is what I *don't* do."

—Lisa Bloom

chapter 10

Lisa,

a "Renaissance Woman" Who Is Living Her Dreams

EVERY FEW MONTHS—sometimes even weeks—I see an article that asks in one way or another, "Can women have it all?" Ever since leaving the solitude of the home in droves to enter the workforce, women have been balancing their careers, family lives, and personal lives, trying to fit all the pieces seamlessly together. I think it's interesting that it's generally women who are perceived to be struggling to "have it all." Based on my experience, I'd say that men and women alike are trying to find enough hours in the day to pursue all the things they want in their lives. I look at Alex, who had to alter how he did his work to be able to spend more time with his family. At Cathy, who worked hard to balance motherhood, an education, and, ultimately, a career. Or at Leanne, who was spending far too much time working and not enough time doing the things that brought her joy. Relatively speaking, and thanks to the feminists of the past and present, women's lives have changed drastically in the past one hundred years (although we're still searching for equality in some areas), but women *and* men struggle daily to find the right mixture of personal time, family time, and work satisfaction.

One woman I spoke with has thought long and hard on the subject and has designed her entire life to make room for all those things. At fifty-two, Lisa Bloom is an author, lawyer, legal analyst for NBC, and former TV host who has found the time to be a mom, run her own law firm, pen three books, read a book a week, maintain lifelong friendships, and travel for three months out of the year. If you're like me, you're thinking to yourself right now, *Can I bottle that?* Sadly, we can't drink a magic potion to achieve her level of satisfaction. We can adopt her fantastic tactics for balancing her time and her life interests and adapt them to our own lives.

When I meet people who seem able to do twenty things at once while I'm still tying my shoes, I immediately wonder just how they can accomplish so much. Do they have more than twenty-four hours in a day? Are they just better at time management? Lisa told me, "A lot of it is what I *don't* do." It seems that much of her secret to success was becoming a "master delegator." She explained it this way, "Before I started my own law practice here in 2010, I practiced law working for other people and I did a lot of drudge work that I didn't like. I was really ready to be done with that. But my fiancé Braden, who is a business guy, said to me, 'You know you can run a law practice like a business and you can hire people to do the stuff that you don't like to do.' I was hesitant, but I gave it a try and I'm glad I did because it worked out very well. I think he's been integral to the success of my law firm because he really keeps me on track to run it like a business. So I have three associates and I have staff, and basically anything that can be delegated, I do delegate. And as my associates get more and more experienced, I can delegate more to them. A key is having people who are very smart and reliable—which I have."

Lisa and Leanne, both businesses owners, surround themselves with capable people. Lisa said she had to let go of the idea that everything had to be done by her. "I think that's a very stressful attitude to have," she said. "There are a lot of wonderful, smart people out there. I think people who are successful in business all understand that you have to have a good team around you. Really none of us is indispensable, which is a very relaxing thought."

Delegating isn't just a tool for inside the office. The reason Lisa is able to get so much done is because that idea extends to all areas of her life. That includes the scrubbing, vacuuming, dusting, and sweeping that needs to be done at home. In her book *Think*, she tells young women to stop spending their evenings cleaning sinks and bathtubs, and instead outsource that work to the professionals or divvy it up among the household members so that everyone does their fair share. Lisa believes that too many women take on housework as something that they *have* to do, when they have partners, or children, or enough extra cash to hire someone who could help ease that burden.

Lisa was married and divorced twice while her children were growing up. As a single working mother for a good chunk of her children's youth, Lisa could easily have fallen into the trap so many of us do—trying to take care of everything like working, cooking, cleaning, parenting by ourselves, and leaving no time for any personal hobbies or a much-needed breather. Lisa said, "I not only worked a number of jobs while my kids were growing up, I also wanted to exercise and I wanted to have girlfriends and I wanted to read books. I've always read about a book a week. So delegating enables me to do those things. I would sit on the couch and read my book or talk on the phone with a friend, and the kids would be cleaning up and doing things."

For Lisa, it's not just about spending her time doing the things she enjoys; it's also about teaching her kids a vital life lesson. She said, "I just think it sends an important message that Mom works hard and they have responsibilities too. We're all part of a team; I never wanted them to feel like I was their servant."

According to the Labor Department's 2011 American Time Use Survey, men spend one-third of the amount of time as women doing chores.[34] That breaks down to an average of sixteen minutes per day of housework for men and a whopping fifty-two minutes of housework for women each day. Don't think that this study just reflects men who work and women who stay at home. Married men with kids who worked full time spent an average of fourteen minutes per day on housework, while married women who worked full time spent fifty-one minutes.

When Gary and I were selling our house, the best gift we gave ourselves was a cleaning service to come in once every two weeks to do a deep clean. Selling a house is difficult enough, always having to make sure every little thing is put away. We both worked full time and found that we were going batty from trying to keep up. We weren't having any fun and recognized that there were only so many hours in the day. If you're spending all of them tending to obligations rather than dedicating even a little time to enjoying yourself, there is no way that life can be balanced. Lisa is right. Sometimes the biggest gift you can give yourself is a reprieve from those tasks you hate. For me, it's cleaning the bathtub and washing floors. And yet, it took me years to even consider bringing someone else in to do those tasks. Why did I wait? At times it was due to financial reasons, but mostly, it was because I felt that since it was my tub, it was my job. Even though a professional did it better and more frequently than I did, I was stuck. Stuck in the belief system that I had to have a hand in absolutely everything. Giving up that control, allowing others to do the work that needed to be done, gave me so much more free time. That free time turned into writing, reading, working out, playing games, and even napping. Money well spent.

Lisa also talked a lot about how her parenting style was very different from many of the people she knew. She said, "I think a lot of moms today really feel like they have to be hands-on and structure every minute of their kids' lives. I don't think that's healthy for anyone. It's not healthy for the mom. It's not healthy for the kids. I'm more of the philosophy from when I was growing up—let kids have a lot of free time. Let them structure their own play. I felt that my job was to feed them, house them, educate them, love them, be there for them when they need me, but also recede and let them have their own experiences."

Everyone does their own thing when it comes to parenting. I have friends who are pretty hands off, and others who practice attachment parenting. As I'm not a mom, I can't speak to what's the best method. However, I do see parents who never ever get a break, and they struggle. They put their personal lives and aspirations on hold for the sake of their children. That's not to say they shouldn't put energy into their children, but there has to be a balance. As Lisa said, she wants her family to be a team, and that means *everyone* puts in time toward housework and *everyone* gets time to enjoy themselves.

There is a lot to learn from Lisa and her decision to delegate in her professional as well as in her personal life. By entrusting others, she's also teaching. Her kids were shocked when they went to college and found that their classmates had no idea how to do laundry or dishes. It was completely foreign to their peers because their peers always had a parent to pick up the slack. Because the associates at Lisa's law firm get the opportunity to do high-level work, they get to hone their skills, which will serve them in the future. As a result, Lisa doesn't feel like she's going to spontaneously combust from all the different parts of her life. My take-home lesson from Lisa was that in order to have it all, you can't do it all. And that's okay.

LISA KNOWS SHE NEEDS CERTAIN THINGS to recharge her batteries. That's why she has organized her life in such a way that she travels three months out of the year. Yes, three months! It's not that she stops working altogether. She makes sure to visit places that have Internet access so she can communicate with her staff in Los Angeles. In this way, despite being a person who works full time, Lisa isn't tied down.

According to the report "No-Vacation Nation Revisited" by the Center for Economic and Policy Research, "The United States is the only advanced economy in the world that does not guarantee its workers paid vacation."[35] They report, "In the absence of government standards, almost one in four Americans has no paid vacation (23 percent) and no paid holidays (23 percent). According to government survey data, the average worker in the private sector in the United States receives only about ten days of paid vacation and about six paid holidays per year: less than the minimum legal standard set in the rest of world's rich economies excluding Japan."[36]

And yet *Forbes* and *Business Week* publish articles on how taking vacations makes us better at our jobs and more inspired to reach our goals. Companies like Patagonia (a regular on the lists of best places to work) actually build vacation time and flextime into their work culture. It's normal for an employee at Patagonia to leave for the afternoon to go surfing, climbing, see their kids, or take a class. Yvon Chouinard, the owner and founder of the outdoors apparel company, even wrote a book called *Let My People Go Surfing*. Taking a vacation, even if it's just a long weekend, is vital to achieve balance. There is no faster way to burn out than by not taking a break to recharge.

Like Eric, Lisa finds learning about other cultures and immersing herself in a foreign country to be exhilarating. She said, "I love traveling. I think it's fascinating. There's really no substitute for it. I love reading books too because I think that kind of takes you into another world. But traveling literally takes you into another world. I'm always either on a trip or planning the next trip. And I'm very lucky. We set up our lives so that we could do this. And we did that by making most of what we do online so we can do it from anywhere. Thank God for the Internet, because it allows me to travel." She has climbed Kilimanjaro in Africa, done the Annapurna Circuit in Nepal, and been all over the world, always eager to explore and unwind.

Lisa's schedule can get pretty tight. Right now, as I'm writing, she's traveling to talk about her new book, *Suspicion Nation: The Inside Story of the Trayvon Martin Injustice and Why We Continue to Repeat It.* This contemporary story of the shooting and death of a seventeen-year-old boy in Florida is an intense subject, to say the least. Lisa interviewed key trial participants and looked further into the evidence, including evidence that wasn't allowed to be seen during the trial. She said, "Right now I'm staring down my book launch, which is in a few weeks. It's just a huge undertaking to have written this book." Not only was the writing exhausting, but she's gearing up for the publicity part. She can forget being alone in her own writer bubble. Now it's time to talk very publicly about a tragedy that got all of America (and beyond) outraged. That's why Lisa is already planning her next vacation, so she'll be able to escape her daily life for a while and take that much-needed break that comes after a lot of hard work. She said, "I'm planning to take off all of May and then also August. So I can look forward to that. I can be away; nobody is going to know me, nobody is going to know my book, no one is going to care. I'm just a person schlepping around a country. I love that."

Escaping her day-to-day life isn't the only perk of traveling or the only reason why Lisa hops in a boat, plane, train, or car three times a year. It's an opportunity to see how differently others handle big issues and how she might learn from them. "I think that traveling is very humbling. Because of geography, very few Americans travel outside of the U.S.," Lisa said. "It's a big world; we're only 5 percent of it. I think that it's important to realize that other people do things different ways. They have their own ideas and many of them are pretty good ideas."

She gave two examples from her trip to Korea. The first was that public bathrooms had children's toilets. If you're a parent, you've undoubtedly helped your kid hover over an adult-size toilet at a restaurant or mall, trying to keep your kid's butt from touching the seat or from just plain old falling in. Wouldn't it be remarkable if every large bathroom in a mall, airport, train station, etc. had a children's toilet? The second example was going through customs and seeing multiple pairs of reading glasses, all different strengths, available for people to use when filling out the forms. That's just thoughtful. Learning from others, and accepting that no one group has all the answers, is a fantastic way to enter any new experience. Rather than thinking, *What do we do better?*, when traveling we can look at it from another perspective and ask, *What could we do better?* When Lisa travels, her mind is open. And because of that, she's able to learn and grow. Michal was much the same. He enjoyed being one of the least knowledgeable people in the room because that meant he had a huge wealth of information available to him to learn from.

However, it's not all positive when Lisa is abroad. She doesn't just travel to places where people live in ways that are similar to the average American. Lisa has also seen unspeakable poverty and suffering. She explained, "There is, of course, just terrible poverty in many places in the world and, when you come face-to-face with it, it's disturbing. It makes you think. It's heartbreaking and you think about global issues. What is our part in causing them and what is our part in solving the problems?"

It's Lisa's question, "What is our part in solving problems?" that connects her to Leanne, Zoe, Emery, and others in this book—that sense of compassion and duty to the world. As the daughter of famed lawyer and activist Gloria Allred, and a father who thought critically and read voraciously about the world around him, Lisa was raised not just to care but to take action to help create a more just world. Armed with those important lessons from her parents, Lisa pursued a life that was meaningful to her. Today, that means working on cases at her law firm that she believes in, writing books that deal with gender equality and racism, volunteering her time and expertise to nonprofits, and opening up her wallet to the many great causes she cares about.

Thinking back to Leanne's strong ethic to never compromise her desire for a better world for the bottom line, I asked Lisa how she ran her business. She said, "I only take on cases that align with what I believe in. If I don't believe in it, I won't take it. And there are very few lawyers who practice law that way. My mother does and I do. I do a lot of sexual harassment and race discrimination cases. I always believe in my cases. I believe in my clients."

That's the good part, but there is some difficulty that goes with just defending those who are wronged. "The system doesn't always give them justice and that's frustrating, but at least we fight the good fight, and we do it with integrity and fight very hard for our clients," she explained. "So that part is very gratifying."

Lisa is on the side of the victim, the voiceless. Everyone in this country has the right to a lawyer. Attorneys like Lisa also have the right to choose which cases they want to take. Would she really want to defend a slumlord? Or some CEO who makes sexual advances toward his subordinates? How would she feel going to sleep at night, especially after winning a case like that? Probably not so great, and definitely not so balanced. "I don't know how you could live that way. I mean, your ethics are your ethics. They don't change from one situation to another," she said.

In addition to making sure her cases are in line with her values, Lisa runs her business with honesty and integrity. Like Michal, honesty is a core part of Lisa's personality. She talked about how some people lie and manipulate information. "I can't work that way. I have to be honest. For example, if I make a mistake at my law practice, I'll tell the clients, 'I'm sorry, we made a mistake and here is how we're going to fix it.' It doesn't happen very often, but we're all human beings." As a lawyer, she has also seen how many lies come back to bite the liars in the . . . well, you know. She noted that nowadays people get caught in their lies all the time because everything is so well documented through text and e-mail. Those lies come in handy when Lisa is working on behalf of her clients. Bad bosses don't just harass their workers in person. They also do it in e-mails, and text doesn't lie.

Honesty and integrity are a pivotal part of Lisa's personality. That's the beautiful thing about people who live ethically. As Zoe and Leanne noted, doing something that goes against their ethics makes them feel bad. Why would they ever choose to do that? It's so much better for them emotionally to live life honestly, not trying to take advantage or deceive. Instead, they work to elevate the world and the people in it through their positive actions. The same is true of Lisa.

Lisa believes that living life this way, always trying to do the right thing, makes her better at reflecting on and owning her own actions. She said, "If you live a life of honesty, then you really have to examine yourself because if you're going to be honest, then your behavior better be pretty good. If you're going to lie and cover up, then you can do whatever you want. But I think ultimately it catches up with you. So I'm not saying I'm perfect, but I try to live according to my values."

A part of being true to herself means making sure that she's contributing to the world on a larger scale. She does pro bono work and volunteer work and charitable giving. Lisa divides most of these donations between human organizations and animal organizations. But her favorite charities help send girls in third world countries to school. She said, "There is one organization I give to that for three dollars per girl, they educate girls who would otherwise be child brides in India. How can you beat that? So, okay here is three thousand dollars, that's a thousand girls. That's fantastic."

Lisa knows that along with her success comes a duty to the world. She learned at an early age that knowledge is power, so she always gathers the facts she needs to make decisions that align with her values. This means researching the organizations she donates to, living a vegan lifestyle so she doesn't hurt the animals she loves so much, and when she's on television discussing important issues such as sexual molestation, making sure to include information about the issue as a whole rather than just talking about one specific instance that happens to be making the news. Through her travels, her work, and her

In a study that looked at how volunteering impacts physical and mental health as we age, Terry Y. Lum and Elizabeth Lightfoot found that their data supported previous findings: volunteering does appear to help curb depression, keep people feeling physically healthier for longer as they age, and improves mortality rates.[37] In addition, as we've seen in research noted in earlier chapters, volunteering for a worthy cause can make people feel connected to a larger movement and give them a sense of purpose—all wonderful benefits of lending a helping hand.

extensive history of reading, she uses her intelligence and curiosity
to make the world a better place. It's eyes wide open all the way. And
she's all the better for it. "All the studies about happiness are that when
you are connected to a greater cause, you are happier," she explained.
"Maybe the right word isn't "happy" but you're more *contented*; you're
more fulfilled as a human being. My work is very fulfilling."

Of course being a person who is aware of the atrocities taking
place in the world also means exposing oneself to grief and sadness.
I spoke a lot to Zoe about how she maintains balance after immersing herself in difficult issues, and I asked the same of Lisa. She told
me, "I had a friend who told me a story about a judge in a genocide
trial in a war crimes tribunal who said that every day after hearing
all this testimony about murders and rapes and just brutal, awful
testimony, he would stop by the art museum on the way home and
look at beautiful paintings to remind himself that human beings are
also capable of great beauty. I've always used that as a model. I can get
very obsessive and I have to stop and turn it off at the end of the day,
force myself to transition. Music is a big part of that. I love music;
it's definitely a mood lifter. I also play with my kids and play with my
two fabulous dogs."

I got to see those rescue dogs, Bear and Moxie, during her interview. They were definitely mood lifters. Lisa said about her relationship with her dogs, "I call it 'puppy therapy.' It takes you out of your
head." I recall Zoe saying much the same thing. Lisa said she also es-
capes everyday pressures by talking to friends, reading books, exercising five or six days a week by running, hiking, walking, or doing yoga,
and enjoying the nature all around her. Being active plays a huge role
in keeping her centered. "If I go two days or more without exercise, I
can just feel it in my body. I'm not happy. I feel grumpy, so I can tell
that's really important," she said. "I think you have to intentionally
transition out of the heavy stuff. You can't live your whole life in the
heavy stuff. It's not healthy."

As you've seen, Lisa is an active participant in her life. If something isn't working, she adjusts. Sometimes that's an easy shift, like
figuring out how to delegate at home and at work, and sometimes it's
much more challenging. When Lisa was younger, she said she never

imagined herself as the kind of person who would ever get divorced. That was, until Lisa got married and divorced, not once but twice. For someone who had previously judged others for their failed relationships, she admitted it was a hard reality to swallow when she, too, joined the ranks of the divorced. She describes these experiences as being "just awful." She said, "The first time was my kids' dad and I was very committed to being with him forever and not having my kids have divorced parents. I thought all these people who get divorced, they're just weak and they're not trying hard enough and they don't love their kids enough, and I kind of had these arrogant attitudes. And then when I ended up getting divorced, it was very humbling. I had to revise all my views about other people who are divorced and recognize that I'm no better or worse than anyone else."

It takes guts to re-imagine the life that you thought you would have. When we walk down the aisle, we probably aren't thinking, *This is going to end someday.* Most of us enter marriage believing that we will be with our partner for the rest of our lives. What if it's not working? What if two people grow in opposite directions? That's where the bravery comes in. It takes courage to admit that a relationship isn't right and that if it's not right, it shouldn't last forever. Divorce isn't necessarily a bad thing. It's certainly sad, but it generally means that two people who are living unhappily together get to change their lives for the better. Lisa said, "It can be very liberating, too, because you're getting out of a bad situation. So when people tell me they are getting divorced, I don't say, 'Oh, I'm sorry.' I say, 'How you doing?' And a lot of times they say great because they're transitioning out of a bad situation into a much better one. That's why they're getting divorced, right? So that was part of it, too, both times. I was living in an intolerable situation and I had to get out of it. So once I got out of it, I was happier. But I think it's the shattering of the illusion that you're going to have this life together, that it's going to be forever."

Although it can definitely be liberating for a couple to end a bad relationship, it gets a bit more complicated once the partners have children. Oftentimes, especially if parents let their divorce get ugly, it can have a lasting impression on the kids. That's why Lisa and her ex decided that their children were their top priority. Whatever baggage they may have had was secondary. She explained, "This marriage didn't work, but we're going to make it okay for the kids. My kids never saw us fighting, my kids always knew we both loved them, and my kids say now that it was completely painless for them—so that's good and that's really what we focused on."

The other big thing that helped Lisa get through her divorces? Girlfriends. Lisa is a huge advocate for having close friends—whether for helping her deal with a major life event or when she wants to chat on the phone or enjoy a meal. She said that when she was going through a divorce, the girlfriends she confided in helped ease her fears and let her know that even though it's not what Lisa had wanted, it would be okay. Lisa recalled, "I had a girlfriend who I talked to at the time. I said, 'What if I'm one of these women who get married and divorced six times?' and she said, 'So what if you are? Women who do that are no better or worse than you. And so if you are, I'll still love you and you'll still be you and maybe you'll have a lot of fun.'" Those bits of acceptance and kindness helped Lisa not be so hard on herself. Her friendships also served as an outlet for her to discuss her emotions, something each of us needs. "I don't know where I'd be without my girlfriends. They are my salvation. We stay in constant touch. Thank God for texting and e-mail. We can just shoot each other e-mails. I can say things to them I can't say publicly. We're there for each other through everything. We understand each other. I think nobody is going to understand me like a close woman friend." During a divorce, the person you've been closest to for the length of the marriage—your partner— is suddenly out of reach. Having a support network outside of any relationship is vital, both to share joys with when things work out and to help handle the turmoil if things don't.

Not a single one of us is without fault. We're all on this journey doing our best and learning as we go. Lisa said she now knows she lacked the communication skills a marriage needs to survive during her first two marriages. She took that knowledge to make positive changes in her life. She said, "The Dalai Lama says, 'When you lose, don't lose the lesson,' and I always try to think, *What's the lesson?* I have responsibility in both of my marriages ending. Looking back, I didn't know nonviolent communication."

Lisa said that *Nonviolent Communication: A Language of Life,* a book by Marshall B. Rosenberg, changed everything for her and her fiancé, Braden. They've been engaged for four years (definitely taking it slow, as you can see). She and Braden read Rosenberg's book, and what they learned altered the way they communicate. Lisa's bad communication habits from her younger years are a thing of the past. She explained, "I didn't have the tools that I have now. I wish I had. I wish I had learned more about communication. I wish I had learned more about how to work through tough things with a partner, honestly and respectfully. Neither of my husbands nor I had those skills. I almost feel like when people get married, they should have to take classes to learn these skills because the good news is you can learn them and it makes a big, big difference. So Braden and I have learned them and we have a good relationship as a result."

Communication skills. Emery and Elaine have them. Alex and Alicia have them. So do Cathy and Michael. When I asked the key to the longevity of each of their marriages, these people noted that communication was at the top of the list. No exceptions. Now, here is Lisa, someone who has gone through two divorces, talking about how her lack of communication skills early on was a major factor in the disintegration of both of her marriages. Additionally, developing those essential skills with Braden contributes to their current relationship success. If that's not a big enough reason to go out there and work on patience, win-win solutions, verbal support, showing affection (nonverbal communication is just as important), and never raising your voice (it can be done), I don't know what is. I love that Lisa shows that these are skills that can be learned. We can practice them every single day. When things get stressful in the home, we don't have to take our stress out on others. If our partner does something that offends us, we can talk to him or her about it. The thing to remember about communication is that it takes two. I love what Lisa and Braden did. They both read the same book and then implemented the same tactics to better their communication strategies. Genius.

Communication isn't the only tool Lisa has at her disposal to help ensure the success of her relationship. She and Braden have joined their lives together while maintaining separate interests and activities. Lisa, much like Cathy, does not depend on her significant other to meet all her needs. She told me, "Your husband is a lot of important things but he's not everything. Braden is not much interested in writing or literature, but that's fine. I have friends who are, so I can talk to them about it." She said that when Braden headed to a conference on a topic Lisa had little interest in, Internet domain investing, many of the men he knew brought their wives. They asked him upon his arrival, "Where is Lisa?" He responded, "Why would Lisa be here? She's not interested in this stuff."

The two of them are secure enough in their relationship that they don't need to be attached at the hip. If they both like something, they do it together. If just one person is into it, they find a friend to go with instead. A friend of mine told me a story once about how a college girlfriend would cry when he wanted to go out with friends on Friday nights. He would go anyway, knowing that it was important for him to have independent time with his friends. It wasn't without a scene taking place every single week. She was young, a freshman in college, so she at least had that excuse. (And she's definitely grown up since then.) But some people never seem to leave that stage of immaturity, and they continuously feel the need to attach themselves to everything their partner does rather than building and maintaining a fulfilling life outside the relationship. Some even try to guilt their partners into staying home when they could be out doing something independently. Lisa would have none of that. She prides herself on her many worlds, and said she views her relationship as one world independent of the others.

Lisa and Braden are both busy people with a lot of interests. Their strong communication skills help them stay close even when they are apart. It's not as if someone just drops off the radar. Instead, each is aware of the other person's actions and is supportive of them. Like Lisa, I'm thrilled when Gary has plans with friends and vice versa. We find that doing things apart gives us even more to talk about when we're together.

DURING MY TALK WITH LISA, I just kept thinking to myself, *What a put-together and confident woman she is. She knows what she wants and makes it happen. Three books in three years, daily television appearances, her own law practice, and one-fourth of the year traveling with her partner.* I was very interested in her path, especially as a fellow writer. She studied writing in college and always wanted to write, yet her first book, *Think*, was published when she was forty-nine years old. So why did it take so long for her to put her pen to paper? Like so many people, self-doubt took hold for quite some time, leaving Lisa feeling insecure about her abilities. And those insecurities stopped her from doing what she wanted to do.

She told me, "Let's be honest. I think I'm good at some things, and I'm terrible at practically everything else. I will never write like John Updike. I mean, I never will for the rest of my life. You can pull a paragraph out of any of his books—I will never write that well." She said the fact that she didn't think she could live up to those (insane) standards stopped her before she could start. She continued, "That was actually what kept me from writing for many years. I will never write like my great writers that I revere. And then I thought, *Well, but I can write better than the worst ones, so maybe I'll just focus on that.*"

I know what she means. I will never be Cormac McCarthy, Anne Carson, Wallace Stevens, Adrienne Rich, or any of my other author heroes. And that's okay. I should strive to be the very best I can be, rather than comparing myself to my idols. If we humans never took a step until we were the very best at something, we'd never move at all. Knowing that we aren't perfect is part of what pushes us forward, keeps us learning and growing. Lisa said it like this: "Humility keeps you struggling, keeps you learning, keeps you aspiring to do better. I think that's healthy."

I love that in her late forties, Lisa overcame that particular fear. Writing had been a dream of hers for decades, but she had never allowed herself to make it a reality. That was, until she allowed herself to just be the best that she can be. Not the best on the planet. Not the end-all, be-all. Once she gave herself permission to take a chance, she found success. Her first book hit the *New York Times* Best Sellers list, touching people all over the world. She spoke her truth, and people responded. Updike or not, Lisa more than proved her abilities to herself and to the world. Not that accolades are the mark of true success. Even if Lisa hadn't had her book published and had simply worked on a book because that's what she wanted to do, she'd still have been a success in my mind. She dared to challenge herself and she won.

In the first chapter of this book, I talked about Sungrai and how he has no regrets. He is able to live life that way because he always does the things he wants to do. Lisa wanted to write for years, but only when she actually started her first book could she say she was living a life without regrets, with no more fears or insecurities stopping her. Now, a few years later, she has filled her life with the things that make her happiest, just like Sungrai, and is reaping the benefits. She said about chasing after her passions, "You're not being selfish. If you're happier, everybody around you is happier. You're going to be more productive and, you know, you only have this one precious life as far as I know. Maybe we have more, but for sure we have this one, and I think it is very short. At age fifty-two, almost certainly my life is more than half over. Maybe it's two-thirds over. I don't know what the number is. But so I really feel that every day is very precious."

That led me to ask her how she feels about death, a topic so many people tend to shy away from because it's morbid, or sad, or scary. The reality is that we will all die one day. I find the people I have spoken to for this book are more accepting of death because they are living the life they want to live. That doesn't mean they want to die tomorrow. They have reached a level of comfort with the idea of death because of how they *live* their lives. Lisa explained, "I don't want to die. I have a lot left to do. I have a lot of books left to write. And I would love to see my children for many years, and I'd love to have grandchildren. But I also feel like if a truck hit me today, I would have led a very happy, fulfilled life and done most of the things that I wanted to do already." It no doubt helps that Lisa believes in an afterlife. Death may be the end of life as we know it, but for many people like Lisa, it's not the end of everything. Lisa said she believes that "the human soul is too powerful to just be extinguished."

Lisa considers herself to be a spiritual person who has learned a great deal from all of the world's religions. Judaism influenced her a great deal and, much like Zoe, helped shape her overall life philosophy. She said, "I used to go to a temple that was Reconstructionist Judaism, which has the belief that we bring the presence of God into the world through our good acts and we all have an affirmative obligation to do positive acts in the world. And it doesn't really matter what you feel; it matters what you do." Sound familiar? Zoe was told by a rabbi, "It doesn't matter what you believe. It matters what you do." Those words were a turning point for Zoe that put her on course for a life of service. Lisa would wholeheartedly agree. "If you're out there feeding the homeless, then you are bringing God into the world even if you don't feel like it and that's something I can get behind," Lisa explained.

SO MUCH ABOUT THIS BOOK IS FINDING PATTERNS. Out of all the common threads I've found, the fact that good behavior promotes balance has to be my favorite. Living with integrity does more than just fuel a peaceful, happy life. The effects ripple out into the world. Kindness breeds kindness. From what I know about Lisa, her generosity has reached far across the world.

Lisa offered so many concrete tools that can be used toward living a balanced life: nonviolent communication, charitable actions, travel, following her passions. However, one piece of advice resonated with me more than any other. It was Lisa telling me, "A lot of it is what I *don't* do." By delegating housework and work at the office, she's able to leave herself time to pursue the things she wants to be doing, rather than getting sucked into the day-to-day routines. When it comes to having it all, that appears to be her secret weapon. She doesn't have to carve out time for herself. It's built into her life— as it should be.

epilogue

AS I WRITE THIS FINAL CHAPTER, I'm sitting in my apartment in Portland, Oregon. It's 11:30 in the morning in April, and the sun is shining. I did some work this morning for my job at HEART, the nonprofit I adore working for. Then I moved on to my own writing. This afternoon Gary and I will head to the two parks near our home, one that serves as a marsh habitat for native plants and animals (I even saw a great blue heron there the other afternoon) and the other an open green space where we can bring our baseball mitts and throw a ball around together. Perhaps we'll pet some of the dogs as they walk by, chat to strangers, or just read. This past Saturday, as Gary acted in a local web series, I traveled with new friends to the Out to Pasture Sanctuary to volunteer for the day and hang out with rescued goats, pigs, sheep, and chickens. Once the work shoveling compost was done, I sat and rubbed the head of Jimmy the pot-bellied pig as he fell in and out of sleep.

This is our new normal. We no longer allot thirty minutes for this or an hour for that. No more hurrying or fretting over where we have to be next or what we should be doing instead of doing what we choose to do. I don't wake up at night fearful of financial disaster or work so much that I feel resentful. We're living the lives we want, and it feels incredible. I get to write fiction and articles, go rock climbing, spend quality time with Gary and new friends, Skype with old friends back in New York, explore a brand-new city, and do good work at my job, teaching kids about human rights, animal protection, and environmental ethics. I feel like I won the lottery, even though we make much less money and own far fewer possessions than we used to.

Two years ago, none of what I just wrote would have even made it to the page. We had too many financial responsibilities and not enough time for me to take on such a project. We were overworked, tired, and deeply unhappy. The truth is, we could have stayed in that life, too paralyzed by the fear of losing all the money we had put into that house in New York to imagine a different sort of existence. I could still be working three jobs and living an hour away from the majority of my friends, feeling isolated and, frankly, a bit desperate. The money we lost on the house? Turns out it was the best money we've ever spent. Our monthly living expenses have been cut by more than 50 percent. We love living in our tiny Portland apartment with a minimal number of possessions—my grandmother's old radio, our antiques, some books, and artwork among them. Of course, our cats fill up a lot of the space with their never-ending warmth and love. They see us a lot more now. And I know by the happy trails of drool and soft purring as they snuggle up to us on the couch that they enjoy this new life too.

When I first started this journey and this book, I was in the early stages of changing my life. As I put the first words down on paper, I was still living in New York in a house that seemed to only bring me grief; I was working too much; and I struggled with anxiety and sleeplessness. There were so many things that I wanted to change, and I was finally ready to take action to work toward the reality I desired. I didn't feel overwhelmed by the road in front of me. I felt excited and free, like I had finally opened myself up to new possibilities. Holding on to the life that I didn't want had thrown me out of balance. Thankfully, I have a partner by my side who wanted the same things as I did, and together, we learned from our mistakes and crafted a new life that feels meaningful and better in line with who we want to be.

Whenever I get a bit stressed or encounter a problem, I have the very best system for regaining my composure. In my mind, I have a filing cabinet filled with the voices of Sungrai, Cathy, Emery, Zoe, Eric, Leanne, Michal, Daphne, Alex, and Lisa. I have not found a single problem that their words and their wisdom haven't helped improve. My sleeplessness? Gone. My anxiety level? Drastically reduced. Self-discipline? Vastly improved. And my ability to live in the present? That's better too. But perhaps best of all is that my commitment to doing things that "fill me up" (to use Cathy's words) has reached an all-time high.

During my first week here in Oregon, as I stood in front of Latourell Falls, a powerful waterfall within Guy W. Talbot State Park, I couldn't help but feel grateful for the ten people who shared their stories with me, for my husband who was an equal partner on this journey, and for all the people in my life who supported me through this strange and wonderful transition.

I didn't just change the external factors in my life—where I live and how much I work. I changed the very way I process negative information. It used to be that if I'd wake up at 3:00 a.m. sick with worry, I'd stay up, unable to calm down my mind. Now, I focus on my breathing, think of the wonderful things in my life, or focus on a powerful positive memory. Suddenly, my heart rate slows, my skin cools, and I'm able to rest my head on my pillow and go back to sleep. When someone cuts me off on the road or does something thoughtless, instead of letting myself get worked up, I channel Eric, Michal, and Alex. I don't blow things out of proportion; instead I "prioritize" my own peace of mind. Thanks to Lisa and her words about friendship, I see and speak to friends more often. Thanks to Cathy and Daphne, I'm more open about my emotions. Leanne helped me see the importance of making time just for me, even when I feel pulled in ten different directions. Emery and Sungrai gave me the tools to reduce my anxiety over things outside of my control and instead focus on the things that I can change. Zoe and all the others who spoke about integrity helped me live a life that I hope is more generous toward others. Those are just a few examples of the real effects these people have had on my life. In big and small ways these fine people have changed me—all for the better. I do know that if my brain were a volume dial, I had too often been turned up to ten, and now I feel like I'm at a nice even five.

I called Emery a few days ago. It had been a few months since I had heard his voice, and I wanted to tell him that the book was already being publicized online and that a snippet of his story was on the back cover. He was thrilled that everything was coming together and that it would be out soon. I told him I knew it had been a while since we had spoken but, to me, it felt like no time had passed. His words and his story were in my mind every single day. The people you have read about are a part of me now.

I know this pursuit to live a good life is a journey that's never quite done. Like Eric, we must constantly reevaluate the things in our life and question whether or not they belong there. Are we on the right path? Does what we're doing right now bring us joy or heartache? Something in between? Honest reflection combined with the courage to change the things that aren't right in our lives—that's where the power resides.

I hope you've felt the same way—that through the lessons these remarkable people shared, you have found methods that can help you live a more balanced life filled with the people, places, and activities that bring you joy. Change is scary. I know that firsthand. I also know that the only thing scarier than change is maintaining patterns and behaviors that just bring us stress and unhappiness.

We have this one life. Let's all agree to put in the work to make it the best it can possibly be. In the process, we just might create a kinder, more patient, and more accepting world—one we can share and live in together.

notes

1. Mihaly Csikszentmihalyi, *Finding Flow: The Psychology of Engagement with Everyday Life* (New York: Basic Books, 1997), 32.

2. Daniel K. Mroczek and Avron Spiro, III, "Personality Change Influences Mortality in Older Men: Research Report," *Psychological Science* 18, no. 5 (May 2007): 371–376, doi:10.1111/j.1467-9280.2007.01907.x.

3. Daniel Kahneman and Angus Deaton, "High Income Improves Evaluation of Life but Not Emotional Well-Being," 2010, doi:10.1073/pnas. 1011492107.

4. Christopher S. Nave, Ryne A. Sherman, David C. Funder, Sarah E. Hampson, and Lewis R. Goldberg, "On the Contextual Independence of Personality: Teachers' Assessments Predict Directly Observed Behavior after Four Decades," *Social Psychological and Personality Science* 1, no. 4 (2010): 327–34, http://projects.ori.org/lrg/PDFs_papers/NaveEtal2010SPPS.pdf.

5. Jonathan Shedler, "The Efficacy of Psychodynamic Psychotherapy," *American Psychologist* 65, no. 2 (February–March 2010): 98–109, https://www.apsa.org/portals/1/docs/news/JonathanShedlerStudy20100202.pdf.

6. Robert Emmons, "Why Gratitude Is Good," Greater Good: The Science of a Meaningful Life, November 16, 2010, http://greatergood.berkeley.edu/article/item/why_gratitude_is_good.

7. Paulo N. Lopes, John B. Nezlek, Natalio Extremera, Janine Hertel, Pablo Fernández-Berrocal, Astrid Schütz, and Peter Salovey, "Emotion Regulation and the Quality of Social Interaction: Does the Ability to Evaluate Emotional Situations and Identify Effective Responses Matter?" *Journal of Personality* 79, no. 2 (April 2011): 429–67, http://emotional.intelligence.uma.es/documentos/8-Lopes2011EmotionRegulation.pdf.

8. Steven M. Southwick and Dennis S. Charney, *Resilience: The Science of Mastering Life's Greatest Challenges* (New York: Cambridge University Press, 2012).

9. Leslie C. Burpee and Ellen J. Langer, "Mindfulness and Marital Satisfaction," *Journal of Adult Development* 12, no. 1 (2005): 43–51.

10. "Marriage and Men's Health," *Harvard Men's Health Watch,* July 2010, http://www.health.harvard.edu/newsletters/Harvard_Mens_Health_Watch/2010/July/marriage-and-mens-health; Ayal A. Aizer, Ming-Hui Chen, Ellen P. McCarthy, Mallika L. Mendu, Sophia Koo, Tyler J. Wilhite, Powell L. Graham, Toni K. Choueiri, Karen E. Hoffman, Neil E. Martin, Jim C. Hu, and Paul L. Nguyen, "Martial Status and Survival in Patients with Cancer," *Journal of Clinical Oncology,* September 23, 2013, http://jco.ascopubs.org

/content/early/2013/09/18/JCO.2013.49.6489.abstract?sid=87b46b91-6031
-4f48-a8b8-4b4569f58260.

11. Rick Chillot, "The Power of Touch," *Psychology Today*, March 11, 2013, http://www.psychologytoday.com/articles/201302/the-power-touch.

12. Osvaldo P. Almeida, Karim M. Khan, Graeme J. Hankey, Bu B. Yeap, Jonathan Golledge, and Leon Flicker, "150 Minutes of Vigorous Physical Activity per Week Predicts Survival and Successful Ageing: A Population-Based 11-Year Longitudinal Study of 12 201 Older Australian Men," *British Journal of Sports Medicine* (September 2013), doi:10.1136/bjsports-2013-092814.

13. "Having a Higher Purpose in Life Reduces Risk of Death Among Older Adults," news release, Rush University Medical Center website, June 12, 2009, http://www.rush.edu/webapps/MEDREL/servlet/NewsRelease?ID=1232.

14. Malte Klar and Tim Kasser, "Some Benefits of Being an Activist: Measuring Activism and Its Role in Psychological Well-Being," *Political Psychology* 30, no. 5 (October 2009): 755–77, http://onlinelibrary.wiley.com/doi/10.1111/j.1467-9221.2009.00724.x/abstract.

15. American Psychological Association, "The Truth about Cats and Dogs: Pets Are Good for Mental Health of 'Everyday People,'" press release, July 11, 2011, http://www.apa.org/news/press/releases/2011/07/cats-dogs.aspx.

16. "Health; Pet Owners Go to the Doctor Less," *New York Times*, August 2, 1990, http://www.nytimes.com/1990/08/02/us/health-pet-owners-go-to-the-doctor-less.html.

17. Britta K. Hölzel, James Carmody, Mark Vangel, Christina Congleton, Sita M. Yerramsetti, Tim Gard, and Sara W. Lazar, "Mindfulness Practice Leads to Increases in Regional Brain Gray Matter Density," *Psychiatry Research: Neuroimaging* 191 (2011): 36–43, http://www.umassmed.edu/uploadedFiles/cfm2/Psychiatry_Resarch_Mindfulness.pdf.

18. Gretchen Livingston and D'vera Cohn, "Childlessness Up Among All Women; Down Among Women with Advanced Degrees," June 25, 2010, http://www.pewsocialtrends.org/2010/06/25/childlessness-up-among-all-women-down-among-women-with-advanced-degrees.

19. Benjamin Porter, Linda Drew, Sara Haber, Andrew Hebrank, Gérard N. Bischof, Whitley Aamodt, and Jennifer Lodi-Smith, "Learning New Skills Keeps an Aging Mind Sharp," Association for Psychological Science, October 21, 2013, http://www.psychologicalscience.org/index.php/news/releases/learning-new-skills-keeps-an-aging-mind-sharp.html.

20. Bruno S. Frey, Christine Benesch, and Alois Stutzer, "Does Watching TV Make Us Happy?" *Journal of Economic Psychology* 28 (2007): 283–313, http://www.bsfrey.ch/articles/459_07.pdf.

21. Leaf Van Boven and Thomas Gilovich, "To Do or to Have? That Is the Question," *Journal of Personality and Social Psychology* 85, no. 6 (2003): 1193–1202, http://psych.colorado.edu/~vanboven/VanBoven/Publications _files/vb_gilo_2003.pdf.

22. "Satisfaction Beats Salary: Philips Work/Life Survey Finds American Workers Willing to Take Pay Cut for More Personally Meaningful Careers," Philips North America website, May 17, 2013, http://www.newscenter .philips.com/us_en/standard/news/press/2013/20130517-philips-work-life -survey.wpd#.

23. American Psychological Association, "More Sleep Would Make Most Americans Happier, Healthier and Safer," APA website, February 2014, http://www.apa.org/research/action/sleep-deprivation.aspx.

24. LiveScience Staff, "Optimistic Women Live Longer, Healthier," LiveScience website, August 10, 2009, http://www.livescience.com/5621 -optimistic-women-live-longer-healthier.html.

25. Nathaly Rius-Ottenheim, Daan Kromhout, Roos C. van der Mast, Frans G. Zitman, Johanna M. Geleijnse, and Erik J. Giltay, "Dispositional Optimism and Loneliness in Older Men," *International Journal of Geriatric Psychiatry* 27, no. 2 (February 2012): 151–59, http://onlinelibrary.wiley.com /doi/10.1002/gps.2701/abstract?userIsAuthenticated=false&deniedAccess CustomisedMessage=.

26. Janice Wood, "Why We Can't Live in the Moment," *Psych Central,* 2012, http://psychcentral.com/news/2012/08/10/why-we-cant-live-in-the -moment/42968.html.

27. Lauren Schenkman, "Daydreaming Is a Downer," ScienceNow website, November 11, 2010, http://news.sciencemag.org/2010/11 /daydreaming-downer.

28. Sharon Jayson, "Time to Come Clean: Little White Lies Found to Be a Health Hazard," *Sydney Morning Herald,* August 6, 2012, http://www .smh.com.au/lifestyle/life/time-to-come-clean-little-white-lies-found-to-be -a-health-hazard-20120805-23o0t.html.

29. L. H. Phillips, J. D. Henry, J. A. Hosie, and A. B. Milne, "Age, Anger Regulation and Well-Being,"*Aging and Mental Health* 10, no. 3 (May 2006): 250–56, http://homepages.abdn.ac.uk/louise.phillips/pages/dept/research %20bits/aging_website_files/papers/phillipsangermentalhealth.pdf.

30. Jeremy A. Yip and Stéphane Côté, "The Emotionally Intelligent Decision Maker: Emotion-Understanding Ability Reduces the Effect of Incidental Anxiety on Risk Taking," *Psychological Science,* December 6, 2012, http://ei.yale.edu/wp-content/uploads/2013/07/yip__cote_2013.pdf.

31. Medical University of Vienna, "Hugging Is Good for You, but Only

with Someone You Know Very Well," Medical Xpress website, January 18, 2013, http://medicalxpress.com/news/2013-01-good.html.

32. T. M. Luhrmann, "The Benefits of Church," *New York Times*, April 20, 2013.

33. W. Bradford Wilcox and Jeffrey Dew, *The Date Night Opportunity: What Does Couple Time Tell Us about the Potential Value of Date Nights?* (Charlottesville, VA: National Marriage Project at the University of Virginia, 2012), http://nationalmarriageproject.org/wp-content/uploads/2012/05/NMP-DateNight.pdf.

34. Danielle Kurtzleben, "Vive La Difference? Gender Divides Remain in Housework, Child Care," *U.S. News and World Report*, June 22, 2012, http://www.usnews.com/news/articles/2012/06/22/vive-la-difference-gender-divides-remain-in-housework-child-care.

35. Rebecca Ray, Milla Sanes, and John Schmitt, "No-Vacation Nation Revisited," Center for Economic and Policy Research, May 2013, http://www.cepr.net/documents/no-vacation-update-2014-04.pdf.

36. Ibid.

37. Terry Y. Lum and Elizabeth Lightfoot, "The Effects of Volunteering on the Physical and Mental Health of Older People," *Research on Aging* 27, no. 1 (January 2005): 31–55, http://roa.sagepub.com/content/27/1/31.abstract.

about the author

ALI BERMAN is the author of *Misdirected*, published by Triangle Square, an imprint of Seven Stories Press. Her writing has appeared in *Unsaid Literary Journal, Elimae, Used Furniture Review,* and *Puerto del Sol* among others.

In 2012 she cofounded flipmeover, a production company that uses media to raise awareness about important social issues. Ali co-wrote "quiet de luxe," a debut short film that has played in film fests around the world.

When not devoting her time to her writing, Ali works as a humane educator for HEART, teaching children about issues affecting people, animals, and the environment.

She resides in Portland, Oregon, with her husband and two cats.

Visit Ali's website at aliberman.com or follow her on Twitter: @AliJBerman.

Hazelden, a national nonprofit organization founded in 1949, helps people reclaim their lives from the disease of addiction. Built on decades of knowledge and experience, Hazelden offers a comprehensive approach to addiction that addresses the full range of patient, family, and professional needs, including treatment and continuing care for youth and adults, research, higher learning, public education and advocacy, and publishing.

A life of recovery is lived "one day at a time." Hazelden publications, both educational and inspirational, support and strengthen lifelong recovery. In 1954, Hazelden published *Twenty-Four Hours a Day*, the first daily meditation book for recovering alcoholics, and Hazelden continues to publish works to inspire and guide individuals in treatment and recovery, and their loved ones. Professionals who work to prevent and treat addiction also turn to Hazelden for evidence-based curricula, informational materials, and videos for use in schools, treatment programs, and correctional programs.

Through published works, Hazelden extends the reach of hope, encouragement, help, and support to individuals, families, and communities affected by addiction and related issues.

For questions about Hazelden publications,
please call **800-328-9000**
or visit us online at **hazelden.org/bookstore**.